Decorating with Giftwraps

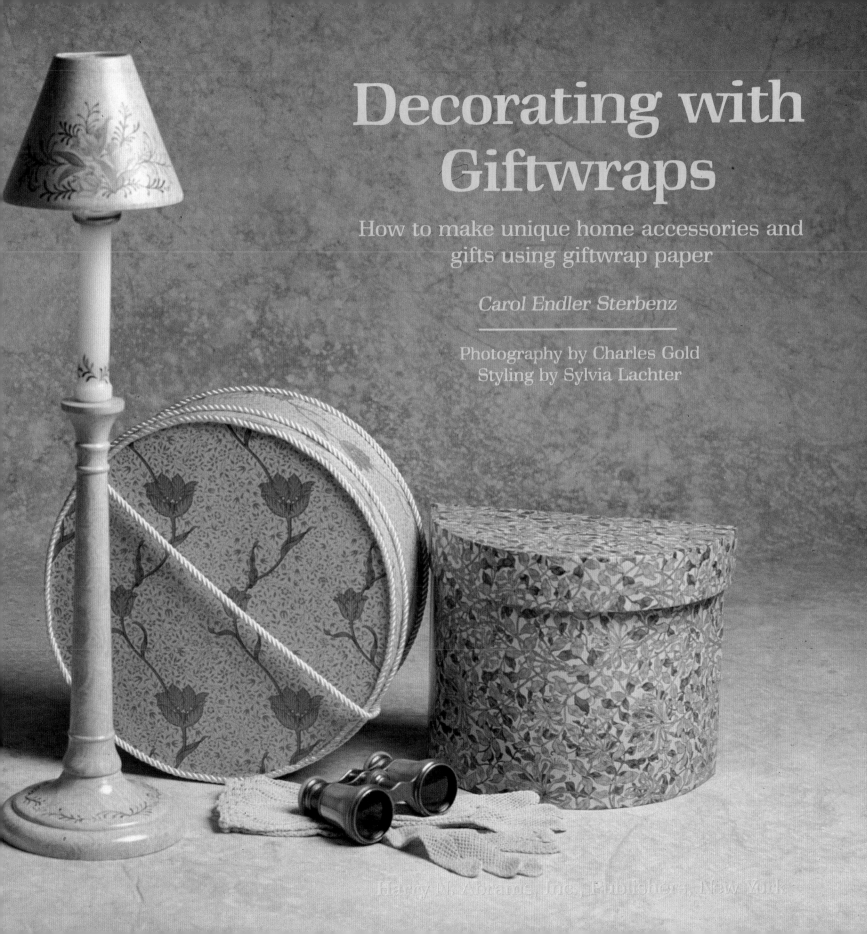

Decorating with Giftwraps

How to make unique home accessories and
gifts using giftwrap paper

Carol Endler Sterbenz

Photography by Charles Gold
Styling by Sylvia Lachter

Harry N. Abrams, Inc., Publishers, New York

To Chris, whom I have known all of my life.

Project Manager: Lois Brown
Designer: Darilyn Lowe
Directions Writer: Eleanor Levie
Pattern Illustrator: Patrick J. O'Brien

Library of Congress Cataloging-in-Publication Data
Sterbenz, Carol Endler.
    Decorating with giftwraps: how to make unique home accessories
    and gifts using giftwrap paper / Carol Endler Sterbenz; photography
    by Charles Gold; styling by Sylvia Lachter.
        p.   cm.
    ISBN 0-8109-2427-7
    1. Paper work.   2. Gift wraps.   I. Title.   II. Title: Decorating
    with gift wraps.
    TT870.S72   1989   88-34858
    745.54—dc19   CIP

Published in 1989 by Harry N. Abrams, Incorporated, New York
All rights reserved. No part of the contents of this book
may be reproduced without the written permission of
the publisher.
A Times Mirror Company
Printed and bound in Italy

The publisher has made every effort to ensure that all
instructions given in this book are accurate and safe,
but cannot accept liability for any resulting injury,
damage, or loss to either person or property whether
direct or consequential and howsoever arising.

Acknowledgments

Decorating with Giftwraps has been a group endeavor, one that never would have been accomplished were it not for the many kind and talented people who assembled in its preparation. I wish to thank: Lois Brown, my editor, who guided me throughout the project; Darilyn Lowe, who created in her design beauty and reason from disparate elements; Charlie Gold, for his luminous photography and unending patience, and Scott Schedivy, his assistant; Sylvia Lachter, who coalesced (and often coaxed out) the magic in each of the projects with her creative styling; Eleanor Levie, craft editor "extraordinaire," who remains the comforting "voice of reason" in all of my books, and who introduced me to the beautiful work of Patrick J. O'Brien, technical artist; Joost Elffers, who conceived of so unique and appealing an idea as *Giftwraps by Artists* that I can be sharing these words of gratitude now; and finally, my love and thanks to my husband, John, and our kids, Genevieve, Rodney, and Gabrielle, who only greeted pancakes for dinner with enthusiasm.

Special thanks to the following individuals and companies who generously contributed to this project: Jonathan Randall of Jonathan's, Jeryl Cohen of Basket Gallery, and Phil Ziegler of The Lighting Place, all of Huntington, N.Y.; Kim Mack of Crabtree & Evelyn; Scarborough & Company; Kelly Freehill of Marilyn Evins, Ltd., N.Y.; Jim Spencer of Polo; Ralph Lauren; WilliWear/Willi Smith; Rodney Torben Sterbenz and Catherine Janet Palmer, of Midnight Origami, Inc.

Supplies used in *Decorating with Giftwraps:*
Glue: Elmer's·Glue-All, Borden, Inc.
Spray Adhesive: Drylon, Borden, Inc., or 3M Spray-Mount
Rubber Cement: Best Test, Union Rubber, Inc.
Découpage Medium: Mod Podge, Plaid Enterprises, Inc.
Clear Acrylic Sealer: Patricia Nimock, Plaid Enterprises, Inc.
Acrylic Paint: Liquitex, Binney & Smith, Inc.
Clear Contact: Con-Tact Brand
Papier-mâché Forms: Palechek, P.O. Box 225, Richmond, California 94808
Glue Gun and Hot-Melt Glue Sticks: Thermogrip, Model 208

Contents

Introduction

When my editor, Lois Brown, first approached me about creating a collection of handcrafted objects using *Giftwraps by Artists*, a series of wrapping-paper books published by Harry N. Abrams, Inc., I was both flattered and inspired. I had admired the exquisite patterns in these giftwrap books that feature classic graphic designs and the work of great individual artists, and I looked forward to exploring the many possibilities of extending the use and application of the papers to create home-decorating accessories and gifts.

Although I had already used the giftwrap in the conventional way, i.e., wrapping gifts, I hesitated at first to cut directly into the paper. While I leafed through the series, however, my reluctance subsided. I began to imagine how beautiful single motifs would look when applied to small accessories and even to home furnishings and the surrounding walls. Finally, I was persuaded to begin cutting when I looked at the William Morris collection: intertwining stems capped by graceful leaves colored in sage-green and sapphire. Sheer harmony! Slowly and carefully I began cutting the paper, saving every beautiful scrap. Design ideas for projects flowed from the giftwrap itself, in a kind of back-and-forth dialogue.

Working with the giftwrap continued to be a challenge and I discovered it was not a fragile medium, as I had expected. Though the paper is subject to shrinking and stretching—and I soon learned the importance of applying a thin, even coat of glue to large sheets of giftwrap to prevent buckling and tearing—I realized that I could extend its durability and versatility by spraying on acrylic sealer or by laminating it with clear self-adhesive plastic (Con-Tact) or by backing it with fabric. Little by little, new design ideas grew out of experimenting with the paper. (Projects in this book that require some practice or experience with materials are noted in the instructions.)

While *Decorating with Giftwraps* is a book of ideas for creating personal enhancements to living, working with beautiful papers can calm and please the spirit. And although learning a new craft and creating something ''from scratch'' can be rewarding, this is often unrealistic given the limited time in our lives. To have to begin a project ''from scratch'' may discourage us before even beginning. I have, therefore, recommended where possible that you begin the creative process somewhere in the middle, so to speak, by searching attics and secondhand shops for items that are beautiful, useful, and affordable, and transforming them into objects that you would love to have in your home or to give.

In her book *The Song of the Lark*, Willa Cather described art as "a mould in which to imprison for a moment the shining, elusive element which is life itself." When we decide to decorate our surroundings or create personalized gifts with our handmade decorative art, we transform our houses into homes and common objects into heirlooms. It is our way of continuing the creative dialogue that started way before William Morris put brush to paper, and it is the most personal way to mark our place on life's continuum—with our hearts and with our hands. It is my hope that this book will inspire you to continue that tradition.

ACCESSORIES FOR THE HOME

The Study

Coordinated Desk Set
Matching File Chest, Stationery
Box, and Wastepaper Basket
Photo Keeper with Coordinated
Double Picture Frame
Telephone Directory Cover
Paisley Notebook

This chapter offers ideas for creating decorative accessories that would enhance the study or library. You may begin with a simple project, such as the Paisley Notebook, or you may feel more ambitious and create the Coordinated Desk Set. I frequently used *William Morris* and *English Floral Patterns* for the projects in this book, but you may choose patterns to complement your own decorating style. Begin by looking around the room to see what finishing touches might be desirable. The telephone directory . . . the wastepaper basket . . . the stationery holder . . . could they use a splash of color? Leaf through the following pages for ideas and inspiration and then begin to experiment. By scattering whole sheets of giftwrap around the room, you will be able to see what patterns harmonize with your furnishings.

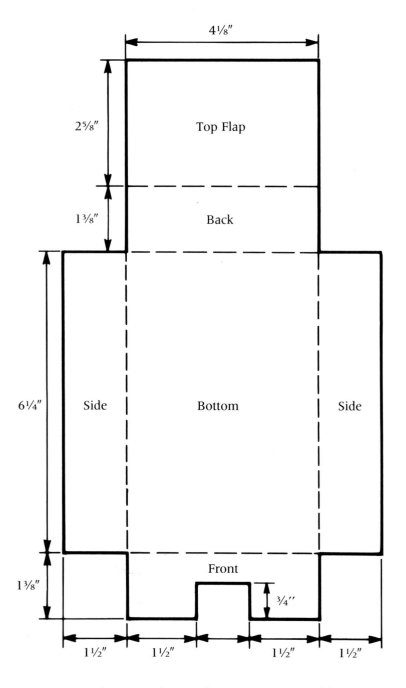

4⅛″

Top Flap

2⅝″

Back

1⅜″

Side   Bottom   Side

6¼″

Front

1⅜″

¾″

1½″   **1½″**   **1½″**   **1½″**

Figure 1: Diagram for Memo-Paper Holder

Coordinated Desk Set: Blotter Holder, Memo-Paper Holder, Pencil Holder, and Stamp Envelope

MATERIALS

Giftwraps by Artists: William Morris
Posterboard
Double-weight illustration board
Blotter paper: light gray, dimensions to fit blotter holder
2 yards clear self-adhesive plastic
Grosgrain ribbon: 1⅝ yards each, white 1⅜″ wide, and blue ⅝″ wide
4″ x 6″ sheets of paper (''memo slips'')
Rubber cement
Glue gun and hot-melt glue sticks
Pencil, ruler, T-square
Compass
Mat knife, scissors
Spring-type clothespins

DIRECTIONS

1. Select giftwrap designs: You will need one entire sheet for blotter holder, another sheet for memo-paper holder and pencil holder, and part of a third sheet for the stamp envelope. Although I show the same giftwrap design used for all the desk-set accessories, you may wish to economize by choosing complementary designs from the same *Giftwraps by Artists* book.

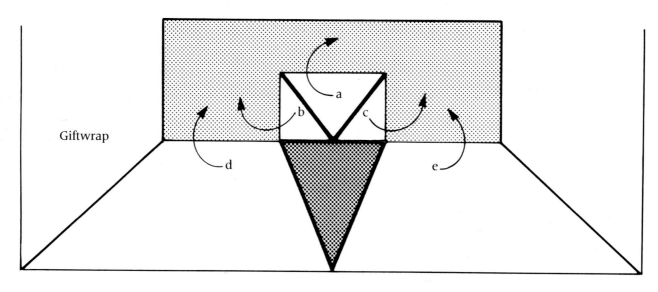

Figure 2: Wrapping Front of Memo-Paper Holder

▒ Inside Surface of Front

▓ cut away

2. Following General Directions on page 95, laminate two sheets of giftwrap with clear self-adhesive plastic, for all but the stamp envelope.

3. To mark pieces, use pencil and T-square on wrong side of giftwrap or cardboard. Cut illustration board with mat knife, using ruler for straight lines. Cut giftwrap with scissors.

DIRECTIONS FOR BLOTTER HOLDER

1. On double-weight illustration board, mark and cut an 18″ x 13″ rectangle.

2. On posterboard, mark the following rectangles: one 17¾″ x 12¾″, two 2¼″ x 13″. Laminate the large posterboard rectangle with clear self-adhesive plastic, following General Directions, and set aside.

3. Place one sheet of laminated giftwrap wrong side up on your work surface, with shorter edges at the sides. Dry-mount double-weight illustration board to center of giftwrap, following General Directions, and using rubber cement.

4. Place a narrow posterboard strip ⅛″ from either side of illustration board.

5. Wrap short edges, then long edges, of giftwrap over to top surfaces of posterboard and illustration board, gluing to secure.

6. Cut two 15″ lengths of each type of grosgrain ribbon. Using rubber cement, glue a length of narrow ribbon along the center of each wide ribbon. Glue each along right side of posterboard strips, wrapping ends to top surface.

7. Apply rubber cement to short ends (top and bottom) of posterboard strips. Fold posterboard strips over onto illustration board. Clamp corners with clothespins until glue is set.

8. Insert short edges of large posterboard rectangle under posterboard strips.

9. Cut blotter paper to 17″ x 12¾″ and slip short ends under posterboard strips.

DIRECTIONS FOR MEMO-PAPER HOLDER

1. Following Fig. 1, mark lines on double-weight illustration board. Cut out along solid lines, and score along dash lines (see General Directions).

2. Turn illustration board over and make the following right-angle folds: First, fold up sides, then front, then back. Hot-glue edges together at corners. Fold top flap over and hot-glue to top edges of sides.

3. Cut an 11″ x 14″ rectangle from laminated giftwrap. Place wrong side up on protected work surface with 11″ edges at top and bottom. Apply rubber cement over giftwrap.

4. Place front of memo-paper holder flat

13

on giftwrap, centered between sides and 1⅝" from bottom edge. See Figure 2. Cut angled slits up to top corners and corners of cut-out as shown by heavy lines on Figure 2. Following alphabetical sequence shown on diagram, fold giftwrap over cutout and front of box onto inside surface of box.

5. Fold side edges of giftwrap over sides of box, making neat "hospital corners" at front, and adhering edges of giftwrap to bottom of box. Fold top 11" edge ½" to wrong side. Bring top edge up over back and top flap. Make neat hospital corners at back, and fold under at sides even with bottom of box. Use extra rubber cement to secure.

6. Cut an 11⅛" length from each type of grosgrain ribbon. Using rubber cement, glue narrow length along center of wide length. Glue both all around memo-paper holder ½" from edge of flap, overlapping ends at the bottom.

7. Cut a thin strip of laminated giftwrap and glue to inside surface of front. Cut a 6¼" x 4⅛" rectangle of plastic-coated giftwrap and glue into bottom of box. Insert memo paper.

DIRECTIONS FOR PENCIL HOLDER

1. Cut the following pieces: From posterboard: one 4"-diameter circle, one 4" x 13" rectangle; from laminated giftwrap, two 3⅞" circles, one 5¼" x 13½" rectangle, one 4¼" x 13½" rectangle.

2. Assemble posterboard canister: Bring short edges together to form a cylinder, and hot-glue, overlapping by ¼". Run a bead of hot glue along edges of posterboard circle and set cylinder on top.

3. To apply laminated giftwrap to box, use the dry-mount technique, following General Directions. First, cover sides: Place wider giftwrap around cylinder, with ¼" extending past bottom edge. Overlap short edges. Bring top edge to inside of box. Bring bottom edge to underside of box, cutting into ¼" extension at regular intervals to create tabs. These tabs enable the giftwrap to hug the curve and prevent bulkiness. Press tabs to bottom of canister. Adhere one circle to bottom of canister.

4. For lining, cut ¼" tabs into one long edge of second giftwrap rectangle. Adhere to inside of box so tabs extend onto bottom of box and short sides overlap. Adhere remaining circle of giftwrap inside bottom of canister.

5. Cut a 13½" length from each type of grosgrain ribbon. Using rubber cement, glue narrow length along center of wide length. Glue both around top of pencil holder close to rim, overlapping ends.

DIRECTIONS FOR STAMP ENVELOPE

1. Choose a note card envelope to use as a pattern. Carefully unseal bottom from sides. Unfold and flatten out.

2. Strengthen desired giftwrap, following General Directions.

3. Place envelope pattern on wrong side of giftwrap and trace around. Cut out giftwrap.

4. Place flattened envelope on top of same-size piece of giftwrap. Refold sides, then bottom, then flap of envelope, bringing up giftwrap as well. Crease through both layers, then remove pattern envelope.

5. Using rubber cement, seal bottom to sides of giftwrap envelope.

Matching File Chest, Stationery Box, and Wastepaper Basket

MATERIALS

Giftwraps by Artists: William Morris; *chest lined with 2 sheets of giftwrap from* Vienna Style
Double-weight illustration board
Glossy black enamel paint
Découpage medium
Acrylic paints: pale yellow (A), pale green (B), leaf green (C), olive green (D)
Gold metallic tape, ¼"-wide, available at art supply stores
Clear acrylic sealer or varnish spray
Pencil, ruler, T-square
Compass
Graphite or carbon paper
Flat and tapered paintbrushes
Craft knife
Glue gun and hot-melt glue sticks
Carbon or graphite paper in white or a light color
For File Chest:
1 yard clear self-adhesive plastic
Small amount of black cotton fabric, 2½" x 2½"
Rubber cement
For Wastepaper Basket:
Cardboard paint bucket

GENERAL INSTRUCTIONS

1. For chest and box, use those measurements indicated in individual directions below to mark pieces on illustration

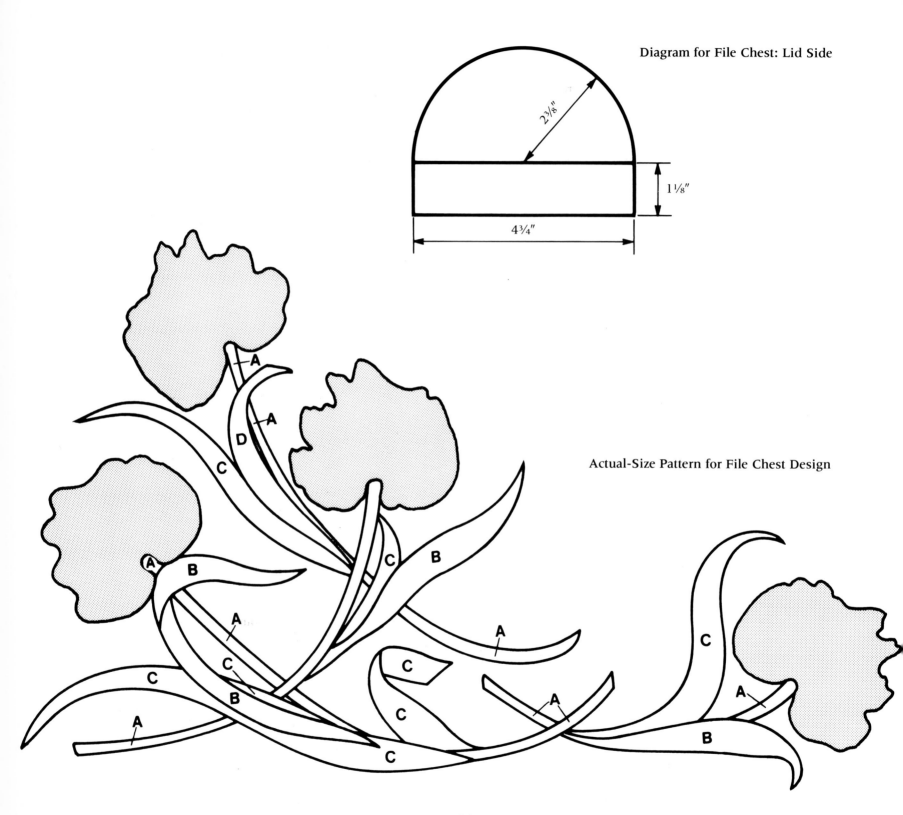

Diagram for File Chest: Lid Side

$2\frac{3}{8}''$

$1\frac{1}{8}''$

$4\frac{3}{4}''$

Actual-Size Pattern for File Chest Design

board. Use a pencil, compass, ruler, and T-square as needed. Label pieces to avoid confusion. Cut out all pieces with a craft knife, using a ruler for all straight edges.
2. Lacquer all surfaces of individual pieces before assembling projects: Paint with two coats of black enamel, letting

Diagram for Stationery Box: Sides

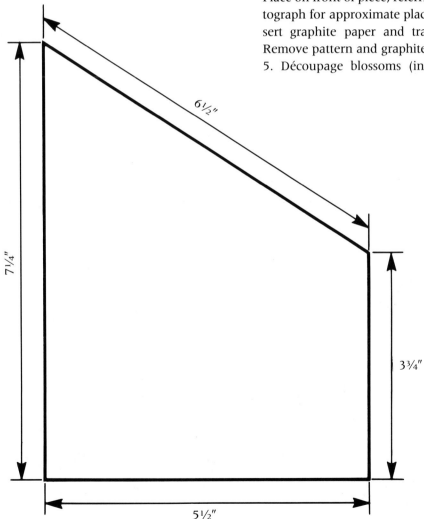

dry and sanding lightly between coats. Assemble as indicated in individual directions, then paint an additional two coats to cover joints and glue. For wastepaper basket, lacquer with four coats.
3. Select a giftwrap with large blossoms; strengthen, following General Directions on page 95. Cut out four blossoms for chest, two each for stationery box and wastepaper basket.
4. Trace actual-size pattern for chest, box, or basket design onto tracing paper. Place on front of piece, referring to photograph for approximate placement. Insert graphite paper and trace lightly. Remove pattern and graphite paper.
5. Découpage blossoms (indicated by

shaded shapes on pattern) to tops of stems in design, following General Directions.
6. Use a tapered paintbrush to paint stems and leaves. Letters on the pattern indicate colors; refer to the materials list. For leaves, blend colors slightly, so that brush applies two shades of green simultaneously; make each leaf in one curvy, continuous brushstroke.
7. Spray finished pieces with two light coats of clear acrylic sealer or varnish.

DIRECTIONS FOR FILE CHEST
1. Mark the following pieces on illustration board: for barrel lid, a 10" x 13" rectangle; for each of two lid sides, a semicircle with 2⅜" radius combined with a 4¾" x 1⅛" rectangle along its straight side (see diagram); for chest front and back, two 10" x 13" rectangles, for chest sides, two 4¾" x 10" rectangles. For lining inserts, mark the following rectangles: two 10¼" x 12½" (front and back), two 4⅜" x 10¼" (sides), one 4⅜" x 12⅜" (bottom). Cut out.
2. Select giftwrap for lining box. Cover giftwrap with clear self-adhesive plastic, following General Directions. Trace lid pieces onto wrong side of giftwrap; cut out and set aside.
3. Lacquer pieces as indicated above. Assemble lid: Hot-glue one long edge of barrel lid around curved edge of lid side. Repeat on other long edge of barrel lid.
4. Assemble chest: Hot-glue sides between front and back, then hot-glue bottom over all.
5. Apply gold tape to barrel lid front, and back of chest, ¾" from edges. Découpage and paint front of chest; see Steps 3 through 6 of General Instructions above.

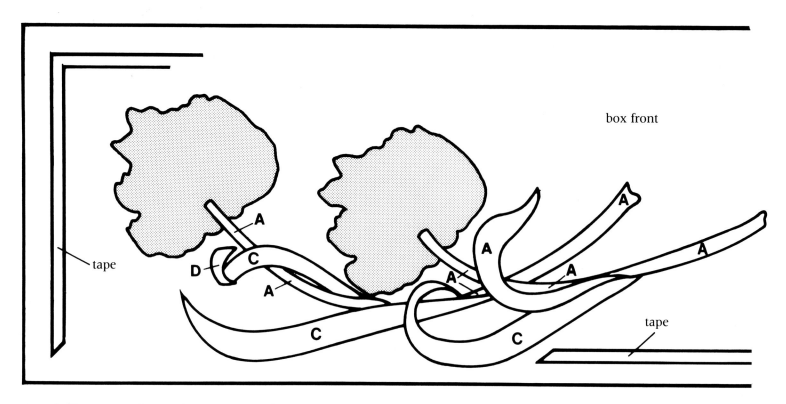

Actual-Size Pattern for Stationery Box Design

6. Position lid so its back edge touches the back of the box, with lid and box at right angles to one another. Place books or other props under and behind lid to keep it in this position. Make a hinge: from black fabric, cut out a 2½″ x 12½″ rectangle. Fold it lengthwise in half, wrong sides facing, and crease. Using rubber cement, glue it along the inside back edges: half to the barrel lid, half to the box.

7. Line lid by dry-mounting giftwrap pieces to its interior; follow General Directions and trim to fit.

8. Place lining inserts, cut from illustration board, on wrong side of laminated giftwrap. Trace around. Cut out giftwrap 1″ larger all around.

9. Using rubber cement, dry-mount inserts to center of corresponding sheet of giftwrap. Wrap edges to wrong side and secure liberally with rubber cement. Let dry. Place inserts into box, right sides facing in.

DIRECTIONS FOR STATIONERY BOX

1. On illustration board, mark the following rectangles: for bottom 5½″ x 10¼″; 10½″-long dividers, one each in the following widths: 3¾″ (front), 4½″, 5½″ and 7⅝″ (back). Also, for sides, mark two pentagons as indicated on the diagram p. 17. Cut out and lacquer pieces.

18

2. Assemble box with hot glue: frame bottom with front, sides, and back, matching edges. Hot-glue sides together, forming front and back corners. Hot-glue dividers between sides so that all top surfaces are flush. Lacquer again.

3. Apply gold tape to front surface of each divider, ¼" from top edge. Add gold tape to sides and part of bottom edge as shown in pattern. Decorate by following Steps 3–6 of General Instructions above.

DIRECTIONS FOR WASTEPAPER BASKET

1. For lining, place bucket on wrong side of strengthened giftwrap and trace around bottom. Cut out ½" larger all around, then clip up to marked line at 1" intervals. Starting at a side seam, roll bucket over wrong side of giftwrap and trace rim and bottom edge. Mark side seam when you reach it again. Cut out, adding ½" to sides and trimming ¾" from top edge. *Note:* To cover the entire exterior of the wastepaper basket with giftwrap rather than lacquer, cut a second shape identical to the first.

2. Following General Instructions above, lacquer bucket. For design as shown in the photograph, apply gold tape around bucket ¾" from rim and bottom edge. Decorate, following Steps 3–6 of General Instructions above.

3. Following General Directions, dry-mount lining circle inside bottom of bucket, gluing clipped edges up the sides. Dry-mount the remaining shape around the inside of bucket, with bottom edge at bottom and side edges overlapping. *Note:* To cover the exterior of the bucket with giftwrap, repeat with second shape on outside of bucket.

Actual-Size Pattern for Wastepaper Basket Design

19

Photo Keeper

MATERIALS

Giftwraps by Artists: Vienna Style
Double-weight illustration board
Posterboard
1 yard clear self-adhesive plastic
*1¼ yards each grosgrain and satin
    jacquard ribbon, ⅜"-wide, in
    contrasting colors*
Rubber cement
Pencil, ruler, T-square
Craft knife

DIRECTIONS

1. Mark and cut the following rectangles, marking with a pencil and T-square and cutting with a craft knife and ruler: From illustration board, 8⅜" x 16" (wrap-around), and 2½" x 27½" (box sides); from posterboard, 7¾" x 6" (insert).

2. Score wrap-around and box sides, following General Directions on page 95: Place rectangles on work surface with shorter edges at the sides. Score across wrap-around 6½" from either short end. Score box sides piece, measuring the following distances from the left-side edge: 6", 13¾", 19¾".

3. Select giftwrap and laminate with self-adhesive plastic, following General Directions.

4. Using illustration board and posterboard pieces as patterns, cut out pieces from laminated giftwrap: to cover box, cut all pieces 1" larger all around. Cut another set, for lining, making box sides piece ⅛" larger all around, and making wrap-around lining piece ¼" smaller all around.

5. Hot-glue short edge of box sides to-

gether, so that they meet at right angles.

6. Center laminated giftwrap pieces over their respective illustration board or posterboard pieces and dry-mount with rubber cement, following General Directions. For the wrap-around, fold right angles at each scorings to ensure that giftwrap will ease over these corners. On box sides, overlap short edges at center of one long (back) edge. Wrap edges of giftwrap neatly to back of pieces, mitering corners and using extra rubber cement to secure.

7. Cut a 27″ strand and an 18″ strand from each ribbon. Holding same-size strands together, glue ends of strands for 1″ to wrong side of wrap-around at center of short edges: shorter strands at left, longer strands at right. Let glue set.

8. Dry-mount lining to back of wrap-around, centering carefully and creasing it into the folds.

9. Using rubber cement, glue back of box sides to center of wrap-around, between folds. Glue bottom edges of box sides to left side of wrap-around.

10. Line inside of box: Cut ¼″ tabs into one long (bottom) edge of box sides lining piece. Dry-mount this piece around the inside of box, with tabs extending onto bottom of box.

11. Set insert into bottom of box.

Double Picture Frame

MATERIALS

Giftwraps by Artists: Vienna Style
Double-weight illustration board
*Two precut rectangular mats, 8" x 10" with
a 4½" x 6½" opening, in coordinating
color*
*1½ yards jacquard satin ribbon ⅜" wide,
in color to contrast with mats*
Rubber cement
Pencil, ruler, T-square, craft knife

DIRECTIONS

1. Use a T-square to mark a 19" x 12" rectangle on illustration board.
2. Cut out rectangle using a craft knife and ruler.
3. Strengthen giftwrap, following General Directions on page 95. Cut 2½" wide strips: three 12" long, four 10¼" long.
4. Hold illustration board with shorter edges at the sides. Following General Directions, dry-mount longer giftwrap strips vertically down illustration board: one at either end and one at center. On 10¼" strips, fold short ends ¼" to wrong side on a 45-degree angle to form trapezoids. Dry-mount two across illustration board so that longest edges are even with top edge of illustration board. Dry-mount remaining strips along bottom of board in same manner. Trim excess giftwrap from outside edges of illustration board.
5. Using rubber cement, glue ribbon around window opening of each mat. Work from the back of mat so ribbon extends ³⁄₁₈" (halfway) into opening, and fold ribbon neatly to miter corners.
6. Apply rubber cement to back of each mat along side and bottom edges only. Place on illustration board 1" from edges and from each other. Press in place.
7. Insert photos or prints from top of mat.
8. Frame entire piece as shown.

Telephone Directory Cover

MATERIALS

Giftwraps by Artists; *one sheet*
1 yard clear self-adhesive plastic
Pencil, tape measure, ruler
Scissors
Rubber cement
Telephone directory

DIRECTIONS (not illustrated)

1. Select giftwrap and laminate as much of the sheet as possible with clear self-adhesive plastic, following General Directions on page 95.
2. Mark a rectangle on wrong side of laminated giftwrap: for width, measure height of directory and add 2"; for length, measure across front, spine, and back of directory and add 8". Cut out the rectangle.
3. Fold short edges, then long edges of rectangle 1" to wrong side. Glue with rubber cement to secure.
4. Fold short edges another 3" to wrong side. Glue at top and bottom only. Let dry, then slip edges of directory's front and back covers into these 3" sleeves.

Paisley Books: Notebook and "Wine Labels" Book

NOTE
See photograph "Wine Labels" Book page 78

MATERIALS
Purchased, blank-page books approximately 4" x 6" with cloth or vinyl cover
Giftwraps by Artists: Paisley
Clear acrylic spray
Découpage medium
Pencil, ruler, scissors
Flat paintbrush
Masking tape

For Notebook corner protectors:
Black fine art paper with textured matte finish
For "Wine Labels" Book:
Small etching, or black-and-white line art drawing clipped from an old book, magazine, or newspaper.
Permanent black fine felt-tip pen

DIRECTIONS
1. Select and strengthen giftwrap, following General Directions on page 95.
2. Lay book on wrong side of giftwrap, and trace around. Cut out 1" larger all around. Repeat for back cover.
3. Apply a thin coat of découpage medium to back of one giftwrap rectangle. Adhere to the front of book, with one long edge ½" from binding and short edges centered over top and bottom of book. Wrap opposite long edge and short edges neatly and tautly to the inside cover. Repeat for the back of book.
4. *Corner protectors (optional):* Use pencil and ruler to mark 4 trapezoids as shown on diagram onto black fine art paper. Cut out. Give each trapezoid 2 coats of découpage medium, to seal and protect the surface. Apply découpage medium to the wrong side of each trapezoid. Place a trapezoid across each outside corner of book, with center of shortest edge exactly at the corner. Bring 2¼" edges of trapezoid to inside cover. Use a little tape on inside cover to hold, and weight the entire book with a dictionary or telephone book until bond is secure.
5. Using découpage medium, adhere first and last pages of book to the inside cover, concealing edges of giftwrap and corner protectors.
6. *For "Wine Labels" Book:* Adhere old print to outside front cover, using découpage medium. Add a strip of paper in the same tone underneath. Neatly write or print "Wine Labels" with black felt-tip pen. Draw an outline around both print and label.

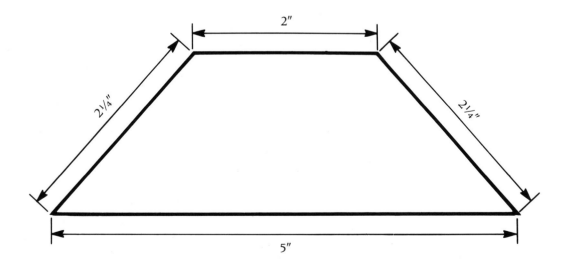

Diagram for Paisley Notebook Corner Protectors

ACCESSORIES FOR THE HOME

The Bedroom

Trinket Boxes
Botanical ''Print''
Small Tabletop Picture Frames
Bandboxes
Decorated Candlestick Lamp
Parsons Table

Because I am personally drawn to the romance of the Victorian style, I created bedroom accessories that reflected the nostalgia of delicate lace and roses bunched in etched crystal vases. The dainty tabletop picture frames, as well as the trinket boxes in this collection, evoke the romance of the past and provide a pretty accent to the dressing table in my bedroom. These small accessories can be easily and inexpensively made.

You need not, however, limit yourself to applying single floral motifs on picture frames. Plan to make several round bandboxes and stack them on a low shelf or on the floor, along with a basket of dried flowers. You may wish to create the smaller half-round bandboxes, filling them with potpourri or fragrant soaps. They are perfect gifts all year long. The Botanical ''Print'' requires great patience but is well worth the effort and will look beautiful in any style bedroom.

Trinket Boxes

MATERIALS

Giftwraps by Artists: English Floral
   Patterns

*Hinged wooden box, about 6" square,
   available from craft stores or tobacco
   shops (these are cigar boxes from Ocho
   Rios Jamaican Cigars, 6" x 6¾")*

*Acrylic paint in 2-oz. containers: pale green
   or rose for background color, plus white*

Glossy découpage medium

Tacky glue

Glue gun and hot-melt glue sticks

Clear acrylic sealer

Cardboard

*Satin ribbon to match background color:
   1⅝ yards of feather-edge ribbon slightly
   wider than thickness of wood used for
   box, or ¼ yard jacquard ribbon ⅜"
   wide.*

Flat and fine, tapered paintbrushes

Craft knife or small, sharp scissors

Graphite paper and sharp pencil

DIRECTIONS

1. Temporarily remove hardware from box.

2. Paint all outside surfaces of box with two coats of background color, letting dry thoroughly after each coat.

3. Select and strengthen giftwrap, following General Directions on page 95.

4. Cut out one large or two small bouquets from giftwrap, for découpage motifs. Cut around most prominent flowers and leaves, omitting any thin, feathery foliage, which can be painted in freehand using acrylic colors.

5. Arrange one large bouquet on center of box lid, or smaller bouquets at lower

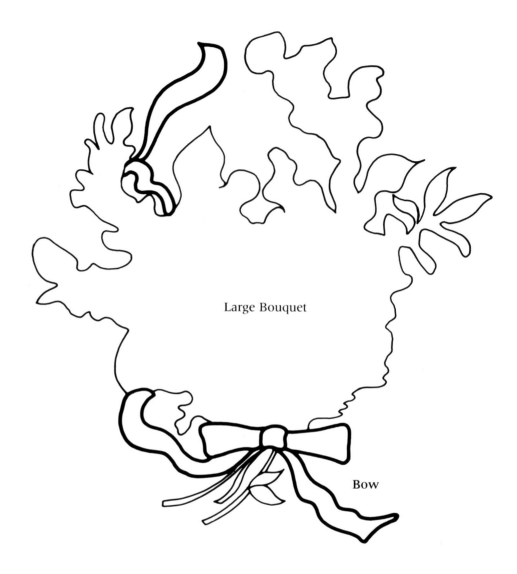

Large Bouquet

Bow

Actual-Size Patterns for Trinket Boxes

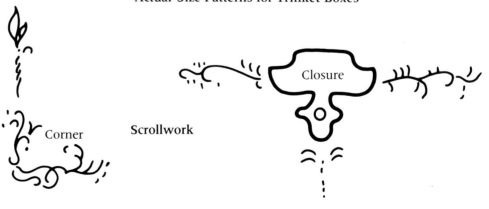

Corner

Scrollwork

Closure

26

left and upper right areas, folding excess down over sides of lid and box (see photo). When satisfied with arrangement, découpage in place following General Directions.

6. Plan your monogram on paper first. Use your design, and our actual-size patterns for scrollwork and bow on large bouquet—either as a general guide for freehand painting, or to transfer first, with graphite paper and sharp pencil. Use a fine, tapered paintbrush and take some time to practice painting on scrap paper: Make thin, graceful lines, comma-like strokes and small dots. Use white paint for the scrollwork and monogram. Mix mauve and white paint without blending the hues completely and use this mixture to paint bow across gathered stems.

7. Spray lid and box with two light coats of acrylic sealer.

8. Replace hardware; see note in Step 12.

9. If desired, attach lid to box bottom with ribbons to support lid in an upright position. Cut jacquard ribbon in half. Apply hot-glue to ends of ribbon, and stretch between lid and box, close to hinges. *Note:* After box and lid are lined, lid will make a perfect easel stand for a small mirror or photo.

10. Line box: Measure bottom and draw rectangle with these dimensions on giftwrap, using pencil and ruler. Measure height of sides and add this measurement to rectangle, all around, then cut out. Cut a diagonal line from each corner to inner rectangle. Fold sides up along inner penciled lines. Brush découpage medium along insides of box. Center giftwrap on bottom of box, and smooth out air bubbles. Press sides of giftwrap onto sides of box, overlapping corners.

With a craft knife, cut straight up corners and remove excess paper from top layer only. Use a few dabs of glue to secure top layer in place.

11. Line inside of lid in the same manner as for box.

12. If desired, glue feather-edge ribbon along edges of box and lid, mitering corners neatly. *Note:* You may need to adjust placement of hinges and closure to account for the extra bulk ribbon adds.

13. To make tray, measure width and length of box bottom at inside edges. On cardboard, mark a rectangle having a width ¼" smaller than box, and half the length. This represents the inner rectangle on diagram. Extend the long sides by ½" and the short sides by ½", then another ½". Cut out the entire shape. Score along dash lines as shown. Neatly cover both sides of cardboard with giftwrap, brushing on a thin application of découpage medium and using strengthened giftwrap. Cut out a ½" square at each corner (shaded darkly on diagram), and cut ½" into tabs, as indicated by solid lines. Fold sides up, and glue tabs (shaded lightly on diagram) to short sides. Press tabs with fingers, or clamp with spring-type clothespins until dry. Fold handles out, and insert tray with handles over sides of box.

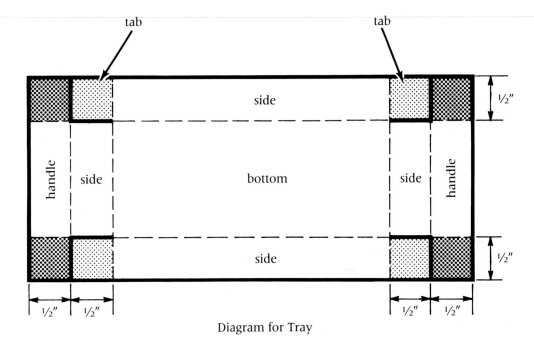

Diagram for Tray

Small, sharp scissors
Ruler
Toothpick

DIRECTIONS

1. Place backing for frame on wrong side of colored paper. Trace around and cut out. Insert into frame, omitting glass.

2. Cut out a vase or urn from a magazine or catalog. Place on lower third of background, centered between sides. Visually plan your design: you will want a margin of space all around the flower arrangement, and a bouquet that will be two to two-and-a-half times the height of the vase and two-and-a-half to three times its width.

3. Lift away the vase, and use a white pencil and ruler to draw a "horizon"—a horizontal line on the background which will be overlapped by the bottom of the vase. Make the line half the width of the background, and center it between the side edges.

4. To glue pieces in place, apply glue in dots to wrong side using a toothpick. Glue vase to background as planned.

5. From giftwrap, cut out sprigs of flowers, leaves, and stems. Cut as closely and neatly as possible. Glue the most solid looking motifs directly above the vase, airier sprigs above and to either side of center, and overhanging the sides of the vase. Glue individual flowers overlapping the top of the vase, and overlapping other sprigs at the center of the bouquet. In this manner, build up the bouquet in a lush, lavish arrangement. Also glue some leaves below the horizon line, as if they have just dropped from their stems.

6. Re-frame the picture, this time including glass.

Botanical "Print"

MATERIALS

Giftwraps by Artists: English Floral
  Patterns
*Cutout of vase or urn from magazine or
  museum catalog*
*Matte-finish colored artist's paper: here,
  royal blue*
Frame
White pencil
Tacky glue

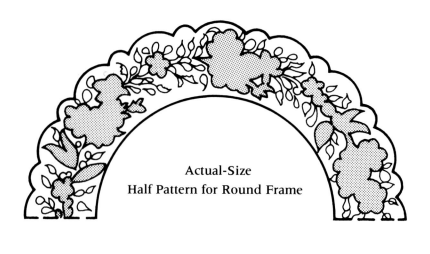

Actual-Size
Half Pattern for Round Frame

Actual-Size Pattern for Rectangular Frame

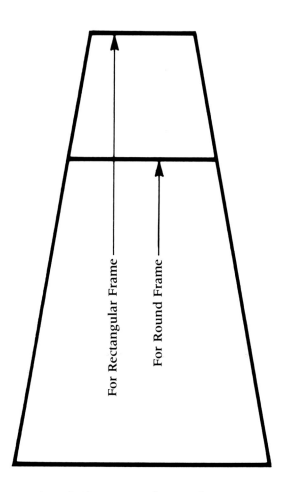

For Rectangular Frame

For Round Frame

Actual-Size Pattern for Easel Stands

Small Tabletop Picture Frames

MATERIALS

Giftwraps by Artists: English Floral Patterns

Purchased miniature wood frames: These from Walnut Hollow Farm (Rt. 2, Dodgeville, Wisconsin 53533): Gingerbread Circle 4" in diameter and Gingerbread Rectangle 3½" x 5"

Heavy cardboard or matboard

Small amount of muslin fabric

Watercolors in tubes: aqua and purple, or color to coordinate with floral motif in giftwrap

Acrylic paints: yellow green, ochre, brown, periwinkle blue

Spray adhesive

Rubber cement

Glue gun and hot-melt glue stick

Small sheet of acetate

Découpage medium

Small amount of clear self-adhesive plastic

Compass

Pencil, ruler

Fine, tapered paintbrush

Craft knife

DIRECTIONS

1. Select a giftwrap pattern which includes a tiny motif. Shown here: small blue flowers in multiples on a stem. Strengthen giftwrap following General Directions on page 95.

2. Following General Directions, découpage motifs to frame: for round frame, arrange six motifs, evenly spaced all around. For rectangular frame, découpage a small sprig or motif to each bottom corner.

3. Using acrylic paints, add small simple lines and shapes to fill in background or unify design. For floral designs, use our actual-size patterns as a reference to paint acrylic leaves and buds freehand. For round frame, mix white, ochre, and brown to make variously shaded little leaves, filling in between sprigs of flowers. For rectangular frame, paint gently curving green and brown stems winding up and all around oval window opening; add leaves painted with a mixture of yellow green and brown and periwinkle blue buds as shown. When paint is dry, use brown paint and a very fine brush to add veins to leaves.

4. Apply several light coats of découpage medium, letting dry between coats.

5. Mat: Place the frame on cardboard and trace around the inner (window) and outer edges.

6. For the rectangular frame, use a pencil and compass to mark a straight-edged rectangle ¼" inside outer edge. Also mark an oval ³⁄₁₆" smaller all around than window.

7. For the round frame, use a pencil and compass to mark a circle ¼" within outer edge. Also mark a circle ³⁄₁₆" smaller all around than window.

8. Using a craft knife, cut out along lines marked in Step 6 or 7.

9. Cut muslin ½" larger all around than mat. Apply spray adhesive to front of mat and center on muslin. Smooth out fabric. Let adhesive dry. Glue fabric edges to back of mat. Cut out a circle or oval ¼" smaller all around than window. Cut up to window at ½" intervals all around. Glue edges to back of mat.

10. Using watercolors in a color that coordinates with flowers (here, purple or aqua), paint inner edges and around window for ½".

11. Cut acetate ½" larger all around than mat window. Apply rubber cement to back of window all around and press on acetate, centering carefully.

12. For the backing, place mat on cardboard and trace around outer edge.

13. For the easel stand, transfer actual-size pattern to cardboard, or trace onto tracing paper and glue to cardboard.

14. Cover back and easel stand on both sides with giftwrap, dry-mounting as indicated in General Directions. Wrap each in clear self-adhesive plastic.

15. Staple top of easel to top of frame backing.

16. Apply a thin line of hot glue around outer edge of mat, as if you were caulking, but leave top edge unglued so photo may be inserted from the top. Lightly press the backing on top.

Bandboxes (Semicircular)

MATERIALS

Giftwraps by Artists: William Morris; *one design for covering outside of each box, another design for lining box*

White fine-line illustration board, medium-weight

Clear acrylic spray sealer

Glue gun and hot-melt glue sticks

Spray adhesive

Tacky glue

Pencil, ruler

Graphite paper

Craft knife

DIRECTIONS

1. Use actual-size patterns for bottoms of boxes and tops of lids. *Note:* While I will refer to these as semicircles, none is precisely half a circle. Place semicircles on illustration board with graphite paper, carbon side down, in between. Go over one semicircle with sharp pencil, to transfer. In this manner, transfer each semicircle separately to the board.

2. Front and back of boxes or lids are one piece, hereafter designated "Sides." Using pencil, ruler, and dimensions provided below, mark rectangles on illustration board: *Large bandbox:* for box: 24⅜" x 7¼"; for lid: 25¾" x 1½". *Small bandbox:* for box: 18¾" x 5⅛"; for lid: 20⅛" x 1½".

3. Use craft knife to cut out all marked bandbox pieces from illustration board.

4. Strengthen giftwrap, following General Directions on page 95, but using 4 to 5 coats of acrylic sealer on each side of paper.

5. Cut pieces from giftwrap, using illustration board pieces for patterns: Trace around each semicircle on both covering and lining paper; cut out ¹/₁₆" smaller all around. Trace around each rectangle; cut out giftwrap for covering outsides of box ¾" larger all around. Cut out giftwrap for lining box ¼" smaller along long edges, ¼" larger along short edges.

6. Draw a line across each illustration board Side, measuring the following distance from one short end: *Large box:* box: 8¾"; lid: 9⅜". *Small box:* box: 6⅞"; lid: 7¼". Score marked line, following General Directions.

7. Assemble illustration board boxes: Run a thin line of hot glue along straight edge of semicircle. Adhere to edge of co-ordinating Sides piece on wrong side, between scored line and closest short edge. Hold in place for a few seconds, until glue sets. Continue running hot glue around curved edge of semicircle, then adhere to remaining long edge of Sides. Hold until set. If necessary, trim short end of Sides piece to butt opposite short end. Hot-glue edges of short ends together.

8. Assemble illustration board lid in same manner as for box.

9. To apply giftwrap to matboard, dry-mount, as indicated in General Directions. First, cover outsides of box Sides: Center giftwrap in place. Overlap short edges at one corner. Bring top edge to inside of box, cutting into corners so paper lies flat. Bring bottom edge to underside of box, cutting into excess at regular intervals to create tabs. Tabs enable the giftwrap to hug curves and overlap at

corners without bulky folds. Adhere semicircle to bottom of box.

10. Line inside of box: Cut ⅛″ tabs into one long edge of Sides lining. Adhere so short ends overlap at a corner and tabs extend onto bottom of box. Place lining semicircle on top.

11. Cover and line lid in the same manner as for box.

12. Spray each box and lid separately with two very light coats of acrylic sealer, letting dry after each coat.

Actual-Size Patterns for Semicircular Bandboxes

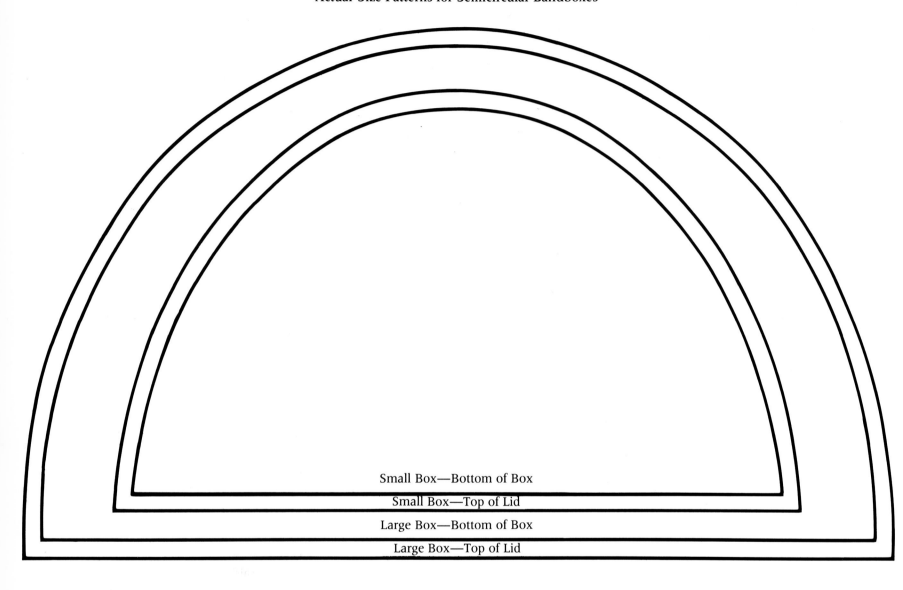

Small Box—Bottom of Box

Small Box—Top of Lid

Large Box—Bottom of Box

Large Box—Top of Lid

Bandbox (Round)

MATERIALS

Gifwraps by Artists: William Morris; *one design for covering outside of box, another design for lining box (optional)*
Round hatbox with lid (to make, adapt directions for semicircular bandbox or purchase in hobby or thrift store)
Twisted satin cord, three times the circumference of lid
Clear acrylic spray sealer
Spray adhesive
Glue gun and hot-melt glue sticks
Scissors

DIRECTIONS

1. Strengthen giftwrap, following General Directions on page 95.
2. Place hatbox and lid on wrong side of giftwrap; trace around and cut out. Also mark and cut a strip ½" wider than lid sides and 1" longer than the lid's circumference. In the same manner, cut a strip to cover sides of box.
3. If lining is desired, cut a piece from a second, complementary sheet of giftwrap identical to each piece indicated in Step 2.
4. Dry-mount giftwrap to hatbox, following General Directions. First, cover exterior: Adhere strip around lid, with top edges even, short ends overlapping, and excess wrapped to inside of lid. Apply the matching giftwrap circle to the top of box. Adhere wider strip around box, with ¼" extending at top and bottom. Clip into this ¼" at ½" intervals, for tabs, to avoid bulky folds. Then wrap tabs to inside and bottom of box. Adhere the matching giftwrap circle to the bottom of the box.
5. Optional: Line lid and box as follows, using the same dry-mount technique: Place rectangular strip around inside of lid, ⅛" from rim. Clip into excess and glue tabs onto inside top of lid. Adhere a circle on inside top of lid. Line inside of box in the same way.
6. Spray each box and lid separately with two light coats of acrylic sealer, letting dry after each coat.
7. Hot-glue twisted cord around top and bottom of lid sides, and around bottom of box; butt ends neatly.

Decorated Candlestick Lamp

MATERIALS

Giftwraps by Artists: English Floral Patterns
Purchased, candlestick lamp
Découpage medium
Scissors, craft knife
Flat paintbrush
Acrylic paint

DIRECTIONS FOR CANDLESTICK LAMP

1. Select giftwrap with small motifs; strengthen following General Directions on page 95.
2. Cut out several small sprigs or motifs. Découpage around lamp shade and base of candlestick, following General Directions.
3. Paint details between small motifs to unify design. Allow paint to dry.

Parsons Table

MATERIALS

Giftwraps by Artists: William Morris.
You will need several sheets of the same design (amount depending on size of table); to economize, use different, complementary designs—see suggestions below
Small, straight-lined table in plastic or wood
Découpage medium
Clear varnish, shellac, or polyurethane
Flat paintbrush
Fine sandpaper (optional)

DIRECTIONS

1. Select and strengthen giftwrap, following General Directions on page 95.
2. To economize, plan an arrangement of various patterns: use strips and squares to create a pattern of concentric squares, stripes, or a random design. Cut sheets slightly larger than dimensions of tabletop, apron, and legs as needed, so pieces overlap.
3. Découpage pieces to table, following General Directions. Adhere edges to adjacent surfaces or wrap to the underside of table. Avoid folding giftwrap under itself; instead, cut away excess paper.
4. Apply at least two coats of a sealer, such as varnish. For optimal results, apply 4 to 5 coats, sanding lightly between coats.

ACCESSORIES FOR THE HOME

The Living Room

"Our Guests" Album
Coasters
Decorated Table, Settee,
*   Westminster Clock, and Wall*
*   Border*
Fringed Floorcloth
Pleated Lamp Shade
Landscape Rabbit
Three-Dimensional Artwork
Origami Fish

A simple and effective way to enhance a living room is by creating a decorative wall border. Using motifs from any of the giftwrap patterns, you can apply them to the wall just below the ceiling, or follow around the windows and doors, or highlight a fireplace mantel or chair rail. For my living room, I combined several pieces of neutral-colored furniture: a honey-colored library table, a ladder-back chair, and a Westminster clock. To unify them, I added a narrative border of irises and wrens and lined the interior cabinet of the clock with sheets of William Morris' "Willow Boughs." A fringed floor-cloth with a basket of baby's breath finished off the setting.

How often do we discover a special object that simply delights us "as is"? Such was the inspiration for the Landscape Rabbit. I was enchanted by the idea of creating a kind of "trompe l'oeil" landscape at the base of the papier-mâché rabbit.

The Three-Dimensional Artwork offered a unique opportunity for me to try something new, to create a standing sculpture using the giftwrap. I must admit that I had expert help. After creating the "ocean," I simply consulted Rodney, my son, and Catherine Palmer, a friend of my daughter Genevieve, to come up with an accessory that would be conceptually related to the standing sculpture. The Origami Fish were their solution.

Albums: "Our Guests" and "Our Wedding"

NOTE
See photograph "Our Wedding" Album page 74

MATERIALS
Giftwraps by Artists: *William Morris and English Floral Patterns*
Purchased blank-sheet book, either paperback ("Our Guests"—10" x 8") or cloth-covered hardbound ("Our Wedding"—14" x 10")
Flint paper (available at art supply stores) in color to coordinate with cover of giftwrap book
Clear acetate sheets
Grosgrain ribbon in coordinating color
Watercolors in tubes: white, color to match background of giftwrap; pink and green (optional)
White press-type lettering, ⅝" high
Spray adhesive
Rubber cement
Tracing paper
Graphite paper
Pencil, ruler
Craft knife
Fine, tapered paintbrush

DIRECTIONS FOR PAPERBACK ALBUM
1. For inside covers and flyleaves (sheet of paper at the beginning and end of al-

bum), select and strengthen giftwrap paper, following General Directions on page 95.

2. Open out covers and place book face down on giftwrap; trace around. Mark where binding occurs at top and bottom of giftwrap; remove book and connect marked points with a ruled line. Cut one half (which will fit over inside cover) ½" larger all around; cut the opposite half (flyleaf) along marked line. Cut an identical sheet of giftwrap, for back inside cover and flyleaf.

3. Dry-mount giftwrap to inside of front cover, following General Directions, and folding edges of giftwrap over ½" onto front covers. Leave flyleaf side of giftwrap unattached. Repeat for back inside cover and flyleaf.

4. From grosgrain ribbon, cut two strands each measuring 2" longer than width of book. Glue end of one strand to front of book at center of right edge, with ribbon extending to the right. Glue end of second strand to back of book at center of left edge, with ribbon extending to the left. Trim free ribbon ends on an angle. When album is completed, tie ribbons together in a bow.

5. Remove cover in one piece from giftwrap book.

6. Place cover on a protected surface, and use craft knife to cut out just inside the oval, arch, and/or rectangle which enclose the book title on front and book information and UPC code on back, forming "windows." Cut carefully around any prominent shapes which extend into these areas.

7. Wrap cover around the softback book so that bindings match and a prominent window is centered between top and bottom edges on front of book. Open book out and trace around book onto cover. Remove cover. Using ruler and craft knife, cut out cover slightly to the inside of marked line.

8. Cut flint paper and plastic sheet 1" larger all around than window. Temporarily center flint paper behind window opening. Trace and transfer one of the titles shown here to the flint paper, using carbon or graphite paper and centering carefully in the window of the cover. Using fine, tapered paintbrush and white paint, go over marked lettering. If desired, add curlicues, dots, or simple scrollwork designs in keeping with giftwrap book cover design.

9. For titles not patterned here, use press-type to label the front cover of your album. Follow manufacturer's instructions. If desired, paint little pink dot rosebuds and little green V-shaped calyces over wide strokes of lettering.

10. Using rubber cement, apply glue to wrong side of cover all around window, and press the sheet of acetate in place. Apply glue to acetate around window, then press flint paper behind that, positioning lettering carefully so title is centered in window.

11. Following Step 10, glue acetate and a plain sheet of flint paper behind windows on back cover.

12. Dry-mount cover around book.

13. (Optional) Embellish a title page as follows: Cut out a motif from giftwrap. Glue to first blank right-hand page of book, to left of center. Letter title at center of page, and paint brackets to unify lettering and motif.

DIRECTIONS FOR HARDBOUND ALBUM

1. Choose a color that coordinates nicely with desired cover of giftwrap book. Mix watercolors to achieve desired color. Using a flat brush, paint the linen surface of the book at the edges and binding. Let dry.

2. For inside covers and flyleaves (sheet of paper at the beginning and end of album), select and strengthen giftwrap paper, following General Directions on page 95.

3. Insert a folded edge of giftwrap into book between cover and first page. Trace around pages of book to mark outline onto giftwrap. Remove giftwrap and cut out along marked line; unfold. From same giftwrap, cut a second piece to same size. Following General Directions, dry-mount one sheet of giftwrap across front inside cover and first page. Dry-mount second sheet of giftwrap across last page and back inside cover.

4. Using a craft knife, remove front and back covers from giftwrap book.

5. Following Step 6 above, cut out windows from covers.

6. Place one cover over front of book so that a prominent window is centered. Turn book and cover over and trace around book. Using ruler and craft knife, cut out slightly to inside of marked line. Cut ½" from inside edge of cover. Repeat for back of book.

7. Follow Steps 4, 8, 9, 10, and 11 for paperback album.

8. Dry-mount covers to front and back of book, matching top, outside, and bottom edges and leaving binding uncovered.

9. If desired, follow Step 13 above.

Coasters

NOTE
For hot and cold drinks; to clean, wipe coasters with damp sponge.

MATERIALS
Giftwraps by Artists: English Floral Patterns
Acrylic paint: Light blue, white, red, emerald
Watercolor paints: ochre, lime green, brown
Double-weight illustration board
Metallic gold pressure-sensitive graphic tape ⅛" wide, available at art supply stores
Découpage medium
Pencil, ruler
Craft knife
Flat and fine, tapered paintbrushes

DIRECTIONS FOR EACH COASTER
1. Using pencil and ruler, mark off a 5" square on double-weight illustration board. Using ruler and craft knife and working on a protected surface, cut out square. Round corners: First place a coin at each corner and trace around, then cut along curves.
2. Strengthen giftwrap, following General Directions on page 95.
3. Paint one surface plus edges of coaster light blue.
4. Place coaster on wrong side of giftwrap. Trace around, and cut out. Using découpage medium, glue to back of coaster.
5. To paint front of coaster: For clouds, smudge some white paint over the light blue, using an almost-dry brush plus fingers; aim for a very light, wispy effect.

6. Referring to photograph but working freehand, paint fronds, stems, leaves, and tendrils on coaster. Use ochre, lime green and brown watercolors, blending paints only slightly. Work from the bottom up over half of coaster, extending a little of the greenery into top half.
7. Paint birds in the sky: With emerald paint and an almost-dry, very fine-line brush, make a couple of wide angle V shapes on top half of coaster.
8. From giftwrap, cut out small blossoms, sprigs, and even birds. Following General Directions, découpage over painted foliage. Refer to photograph for placement suggestions.

9. Mix a tiny bit of red paint with white and dab around découpaged flowers at the base of foliage.
10. Apply gold tape to each side of coaster, ¼" from edges. Overlap corners neatly.
11. Brush on at least three light coats of découpage medium over front, then back of coaster, letting dry thoroughly after each coat.

Note: To cover entire coaster with giftwrap, follow Step 4, cutting two squares instead of one. When cutting square for top of coaster, position cutout square over desired pattern of giftwrap.

Decorated Table, Settee, Westminster Clock, and Wall Border

NOTE

Prepare unpainted furniture by sealing; see Step 3 below.

MATERIALS

Giftwraps by Artists: William Morris *and* English Floral Patterns
Découpage medium
Clear varnish, shellac, polyurethane, or acrylic spray sealer
Enamel paint: light and dark olive (optional)
Small, sharp scissors
Flat and fine, tapered paintbrushes

DIRECTIONS

1. Select a giftwrap with small repeated motifs and strengthen, following General Directions on page 95.
2. Cut out several small motifs. Apply to clock, furniture, and wall using découpage medium. (For wall border, consider applying motifs to a purchased paper wallpaper border rather than working directly on the wall.)
3. For furniture, apply at least three coats of clear shellac, varnish, or polyurethane. On wallpaper borders, apply clear acrylic spray.
4. If desired, expand the design with paint, mixed to match the leaves and stems of the giftwrap motifs. For example, on the settee, I painted in extra leaves to follow the contour of the arm. On your project, you might add larger leaves, longer stems, or a vine which connects and unifies the design elements. Also consider a straight or scalloped line in a matching or contrasting color, above and below a row of motifs.
5. For clock, I recommend a Westminster clock with pendulum. Open door and line the interior cabinet, dry-mounting giftwrap to all surfaces following General Directions.

Fringed Floorcloth

NOTE

Requires practice applying paper to fabric; floorcloth not for heavy use.

MATERIALS

Giftwraps by Artists: William Morris. *(Note: Floorcloth shown here requires 3 identical sheets of giftwrap. See suggestions below for combining different patterns from the same book.)*
Gessoed cotton artist's canvas, 27" x 54", or size as desired
1⅝ yards wide natural cotton fringe
Clear spray acrylic sealer
Découpage medium
Clear polyurethane or varnish
Glue gun and hot-melt glue
Flat paintbrush
Craft knife, scissors

DIRECTIONS

1. Select giftwrap. To avoid purchasing several identical books, choose 3 or 4 compatible prints and plan a collage design. Strengthen all giftwrap sheets to be used, following General Directions on page 95.
2. Spread canvas out smooth on a large work surface. Plan placement of giftwrap sheets. Adjacent sheets may butt or overlap. For uniform design, lay three identical sheets side by side; match design at edges wherever possible. For a collage design, cut giftwrap into strips or blocks and plan a simple design of repeated stripes, concentric rectangles, or large checkerboard.
3. Working with each sheet or piece of giftwrap at a time, brush découpage medium quickly, thinly, and evenly onto wrong side of giftwrap, and immediately press and smooth onto fabric. Do not overwork, as giftwrap may tend to stretch. Let dry completely.
4. Trim edges of floorcloth with a craft knife and ruler. Apply at least two light coats of clear varnish or polyurethane to giftwrap surface, letting dry thoroughly after each coat.
5. Hot-glue fringe across short edges of floorcloth.

Pleated Lamp Shade

NOTE
Requires practice applying paper to fabric

MATERIALS
Giftwraps by Artists: William Morris
Purchased, white or light-colored lamp shade
⅜ yard medium-weight white linen fabric
Découpage medium
Pencil, ruler
Scissors, craft knife
Glue gun and hot-melt glue sticks

DIRECTIONS
1. Select giftwrap; strengthen following General Directions on page 95.
2. Measure height (H) and circumference (C) of lamp shade.
3. On wrong side of giftwrap, mark a rectangle with a width equal to H and a length three times C. Cut out 1" beyond marked lines all around.
4. Place giftwrap rectangle on linen and cut out to same size.
5. Spread découpage medium thinly and evenly over back of giftwrap. Press quickly and smoothly onto fabric. Do not be concerned if edges are not exactly even. Let dry.
6. Using a ruler and a craft knife with a sharp blade, trim 1" from giftwrap/linen rectangle.
7. Using pencil and ruler, lightly mark lines across rectangle on linen side, 1" apart. Fold along marked lines, forming accordion pleats. Press folds tightly with your fingers.
8. Run a line of hot glue along the crease of an inside fold. Adhere to lamp shade at seam. Apply glue to successive folds and press to shade all around. Bring short edges together, matching folds to overlap them neatly. Trim away excessive pleats if necessary, to guarantee an even distribution of pleats all around. Hot-glue at overlap to secure.

Landscape Rabbit

MATERIALS
Giftwraps by Artists: English Floral Patterns
Purchased papier-mâché figurine; for similar items, write Palechek, P.O. Box 225, Richmond, California 94808, for stores nearest you)
Acrylic paints: light blue and white
Watercolor paints: yellow green, ochre, brown, rose, white, emerald
Découpage medium
Clear acrylic spray sealer
Flat and fine, tapered paintbrushes
½ yard seafoam green picot-edge grosgrain ribbon, ⅜" wide
Small dried or silk flower

DIRECTIONS
1. Paint all surfaces of the papier-mâché figurine with two light coats of light blue acrylic paint, letting dry after each coat.
2. On the figurine only, not the rocker, use white acrylic paint with an almost dry brush and smudge with fingers, creating the effect of wispy clouds.
3. From base of figurine (not including rocker) paint grass, stems, and vines: Use a tapered brush, and varying amounts of ochre, lime green, and brown paints. Keep paints watered down for a translucent quality. Paint blades of grass only over feet, stems extending over legs, and vines curving into haunches. Paint lime green stems and leaves winding up the neck and around ears. Paint a horizontal leaf for each eye.
4. On rocker only, dab lightly with watered-down ochre and emerald paint, allowing base coat to show through.
5. Choose a giftwrap with a small floral motif and strengthen giftwrap, following General Directions on page 95.
6. Cut out small sprigs of flowers, omitting fine-lined stems. Following General Directions, découpage the sprigs along painted stems, placing them predominantly along the feet and haunches, or the bottom of the figurine.
7. Cut out several large leaf motifs from giftwrap and découpage along flat sides of rocker, ½" from top.
8. Using a mixture of rose and white paint, dab on small circles around base of figurine, for tiny pink flowers.
9. Using turquoise and brown paints, blended only slightly, paint a few graceful and wide-angle V shapes over rump area, for birds on the wing.
10. Spray the entire figurine with several light applications of acrylic sealer, until surface is shiny and thoroughly smooth.
11. Tie ribbon around neck of figurine. Glue flower to ribbon knot.

44

Three-Dimensional Artwork

MATERIALS

Giftwraps by Artists: Vienna Style
Double-weight illustration board
Adhesive spray
Pencil, ruler
Craft knife, scissors

DIRECTIONS

1. Choose two different, but complementary, giftwrap designs—the more abstract the better. Strengthen, following General Directions on page 95.
2. For the foreground, cut a 10″ x 17″ rectangle. Recut one long edge following the contours of the design, striving for a jagged, uneven line and cutting deeply into the left side. Refer to photograph for a suggested shape.
3. Place giftwrap for foreground on double-weight illustration board. Trace around. Cut out, using a ruler and craft knife.
4. Following General Directions, dry-mount giftwrap to matching illustration board.
5. For the background, cut a 13″ x 17″ rectangle. Following Steps 2, 3, and 4, cut and mount the same as for foreground.
6. For assembly tabs, cut two 1¼″ x 4″ rectangles from illustration board. Following General Directions, score each crosswise down the center. Place foreground in front of background with bottom edges flat on tabletop and right edges touching, as shown in the photograph. Glue tabs in between along right side: half of one tab to back of foreground, other half to front of background, with all bottom edges even. Glue second tab in same manner, but 4″ from bottom edge.

Origami Fish

MATERIALS

Giftwraps by Artists: Vienna Style
Spray adhesive
Craft glue
Nylon thread
Pencil, ruler, T-square, scissors
Small sewing needle

DIRECTIONS

1. Cut two 10″ squares of giftwrap. Following General Directions on page 95, dry-mount them together with wrong sides facing. Trim square to 9″, using T-square to make sure corners are true. Following Fig. 1, fold square diagonally in half. Bring edges to meet fold as shown, crease, then unfold. Repeat on the opposite side.
2. See Fig. 2: Fold square diagonally in half in the other direction. Bring corners at the sides in to the center. Fold corners out again two-thirds of the way, forming small triangles.
3. See Fig. 3: Push in the midpoint of each side of triangle to nearly meet each other. Flatten paper to resemble Fig. 4.
4. Following Fig. 4, fold shape lengthwise in half, enclosing all but the tips of the triangles.
5. Following Fig. 5, fold one corner up along dash line, and fold other corner back along dotted line. Shape should now resemble Fig. 6.
6. Fig. 6: Pull the tiny triangles in the center out and away from each other, then flatten the entire piece; you should have a shape resembling Fig. 7.
7. Following Fig. 7, pull the bottom corner straight up and hold it perpendicular to the rest of the shape. Place a couple of fingers inside and open it up, pulling the sides out and flattening it into a kite shape.
8. Turn piece to the reverse side and repeat. Shape should now resemble Fig. 8. Fold one part of the kite back and to the inside where indicated in Fig. 8.
9. Fig. 9: Pull the opposite part of the kite under, pulling the corner straight down to form a tail fin.
10. Repeat on the reverse side, but fold the top part of the kite down first, then create a tail fin pointing in the opposite direction from the previous one made. See Fig. 10.
11. Dab glue between tail fins to secure. Thread nylon onto a needle and stitch through fish at top center; knot ends to form a hanging loop.

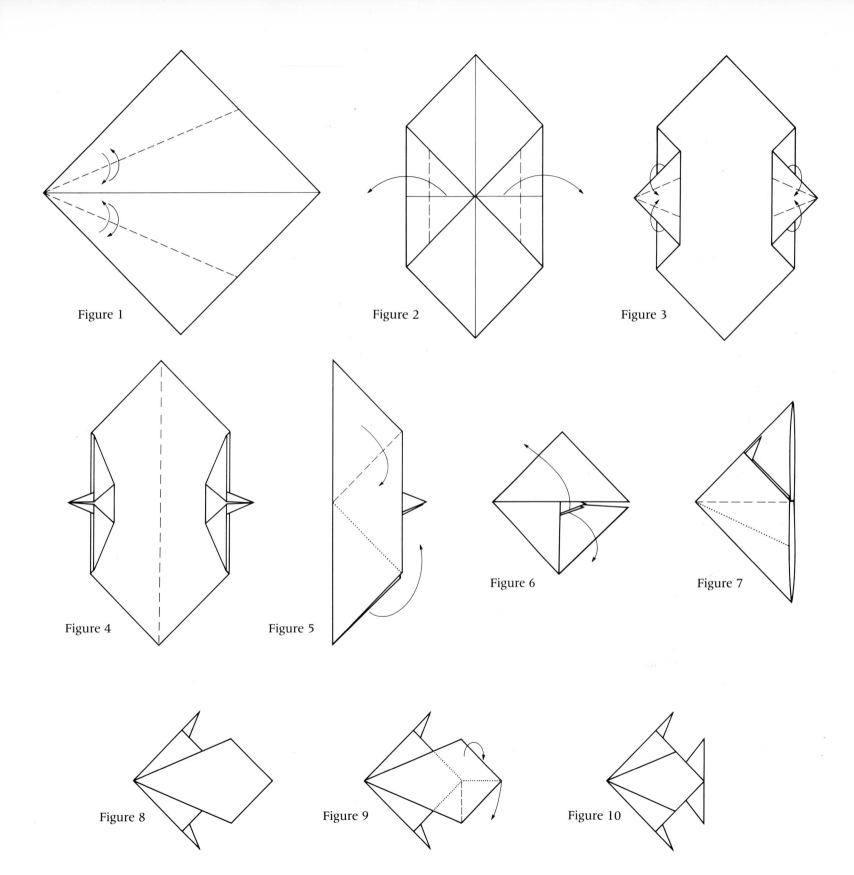

Figure 1

Figure 2

Figure 3

Figure 4

Figure 5

Figure 6

Figure 7

Figure 8

Figure 9

Figure 10

PERSONALIZED STATIONERY

Staying in Touch

Stationery Keeper
Postcards and Notecards
Memo-Pad Books
Triptych Picture Frame
Tasseled Round Box

Few things communicate more about a person than the choice of stationery. Whether you choose to write your message on a postcard, notecard, or a sheet of paper, you can take pleasure in choosing stationery that reflects who you are most accurately and the kind of message you wish to convey. You can personalize store-bought stationery, or you can start "from scratch" by cutting sheets of paper to fit purchased envelopes and decorating those sheets in interesting ways. The Stationery Keeper featured here contains informal notecards and postcards; the memo pads are store bought and are covered in giftwrap from the *Kimono* collection, as is the Tasseled Round Box. It seemed fitting to use the Japanese kimono prints for this project because printing had its origin in Japan.

Stationery Keeper

MATERIALS

Giftwraps by Artists: Kimono: Japanese
  Designs
*Gift box for wine (This one from Tattinger
  Champagne)*
Rubber cement
Spray adhesive
Clear acrylic spray
Cardboard
*Flint paper (available from art supply
  stores) in a coordinating color*
*Grosgrain ribbon ⅜″ wide, same color as
  flint paper*
4″ fringe in coordinating color
Embroidery thread in same color
*Enamel fan-shaped earring, minus the
  finding (optional)*

DIRECTIONS

1. Strengthen giftwrap; see General Directions on page 95.
2. Measure the width (W), length (L), and depth (D) of both box and lid. Use the following formula to mark and cut rectangles for each: To determine the width, add W + 4D + 2″. For the length, add L + 4D + 2″.
3. Using the dry-mount technique explained in General Directions, center lid and box on their respective rectangles, wrapping excess paper neatly to insides. Cut a rectangle with the same width and length as lid or box, trim ¹⁄₁₆″ from all sides, and dry-mount to the bottom of lid or bottom of box.
4. Spray box and lid with two coats of clear acrylic sealer.
5. To make a partition for the box, cut a rectangle from cardboard: For the width, measure the depth of box; for the length, add twice the measurement of the short end to the measurement of a long side. Score and fold into a box shape that will fit snugly inside the left half of the box. Unfold and cover with blue flint paper, using spray adhesive. Refold, and insert into box.
6. Glue grosgrain ribbon from underside of lid, around outside of lid and all around box.
7. Cut a 2″ medallion shape from giftwrap. Adhere to flint paper and cardboard. Cut out ³⁄₁₆″ beyond giftwrap medallion all around. Slice horizontally in half. Spray with two coats of sealer. Close box. Center halves over grosgrain ribbon, aligned so they meet at the seam of closed box. Glue in place.
8. For a tassel (optional), wrap fringe into a tight coil. Sew through the coil at the bound edge with embroidery floss; fasten off but leave thread ends long for tying on. Glue thread ends under the medallion. If desired, place earring finding over top half of giftwrap/cardboard medallion.

Postcards & Notecards

MATERIALS

Giftwraps by Artists: Kimono: Japanese
  Designs
*Clear or translucent heavy-weight vinyl or
  mylar*
White tagboard
Spray adhesive or rubber cement
Small envelopes
Black permanent ink, fine felt-tip marker
T-square or carpenter's square
Ruler
Craft knife

DIRECTIONS FOR POSTCARDS

1. To make a pattern, use the marker, a T- or carpenter's square, and ruler to draw a 3½″ x 5″ rectangle on vinyl. Cut out, using ruler and craft knife.
2. Cut cover away from Giftwrap book. Open out flat.
3. Place pattern on cover, planning a pleasing arrangement of motifs within the clear rectangle. Trace around with pen. Cut out slightly to inside of marked line, using a craft knife and ruler. Repeat for each postcard, avoiding lettering and UPC code on cover.
4. On back of each postcard, use a ruler and felt-tip marker to draw a long arrow across the center, dividing the message area from the address and postage stamp area.

DIRECTIONS FOR NOTECARDS

1. Use an envelope as a reference: With pencil, T- or carpenter's square, and ruler, mark a rectangle on tagboard measuring the same width as the envelope, and twice the envelope's length.
2. Cut out the rectangle with a ruler and craft knife; use as a pattern to mark several more on tagboard, and cut out.
3. Fold each rectangle crosswise in half. Crease the fold sharply.
4. Strengthen desired giftwrap, as indicated in General Directions on page 95.
5. Lay folded tagboard rectangle on giftwrap; trace around and cut out giftwrap for the cover of the notecard.

6. Dry-mount giftwrap to cover of note-card, following General Directions.

7. Using a ruler and craft knife, trim ⅛" from all cut sides of the notecard.

Memo-Pad Books

MATERIALS

Giftwraps by Artists: Kimono: Japanese
  Designs *and* Vienna Style
*Notepads, approximately 4" x 6" for Tiered
  Memo Pad and 5⅜" x 8¼" for Simple
  Memo Pad*
Rubber cement
Grosgrain ribbon, ⅜" wide, ¼ yard
2 small, self-gripping (Velcro) tab fasteners
Craft knife

DIRECTIONS FOR TIERED MEMO PAD

1. Select giftwrap: I used 4 different designs. Strengthen giftwrap as indicated in General Directions, on page 95. (You will also use the cover of a giftwrap book.)

2. Place notepad face down on giftwrap. Using a craft knife, cut neatly and tightly around notepad. Repeat 3 more times.

3. For tiered effect, divide notepad into 4 roughly equal sections. Dry-mount giftwrap to front page of each section following General Directions. Insert giftwrap as far into the binding as it will go, taking care to match side edges.

4. Place a sheet of plexiglass or heavy cardboard under first (top) section. Mark a line 1⅛" from bottom of top page. Cut along this line, using ruler and craft knife to cut through a few pages at a time until

first section is neatly and cleanly cut through.

5. Working from the front of the notepad to the back, trim pages of second section ¾" shorter, third section ⅜" shorter. Leave fourth section intact.

6. Cut a rectangle from tagboard to same width as notepad and long enough to wrap lengthwise all around it, adding 2" for closure flap. Place one short end over front, even with edges of bottom section. Score at binding and fold around notepad; flap will extend beyond edges of bottom stack. Trim the flap to 1¼".

7. Using tagboard as a pattern, cut a same-size rectangle from design area of cover stock. To avoid lettering, UPC code, and binding areas, cut in two pieces, planning carefully so they will butt at back binding.

8. Apply rubber cement to binding of notepads and apply tagboard cover.

9. Optional: Wrap grosgrain ribbon widthwise around rectangle cut from cover stock, so it appears on front 1" from binding.

10. Using rubber cement, dry-mount cover stock rectangle to tagboard rectangle, following General Directions.

11. Fold flap extension up and over front. Distance between first and second folds should be equivalent to width of binding. Crease folds.

12. Glue self-gripping fasteners to front corners of memo-pad book, and to wrong side of flap to correspond.

DIRECTIONS FOR SIMPLE MEMO PAD

1. From front and back covers of Giftwrap book, cut and piece a rectangle having same width as notepad and long

enough to fit lengthwise around notepad: Plan placement to avoid lettering, UPC code, and binding areas of cover, and cut in two pieces which will butt at back binding.

2. Place one short end over front, even with bottom edges of pages. Score shallowly at binding and fold snugly around notepad.

3. Apply rubber cement to binding of notepad and glue cover pieces around it.

Triptych Picture Frame

MATERIALS

Giftwraps by Artists: Kimono: Japanese
    Designs
Double-weight illustration board
Posterboard
Clear plastic or acetate sheet, 8½" x 11"
Glossy black enamel paint
Metallic gold pressure-sensitive graphic
    tape, ⅛" wide, available at art supply
    stores
Gold leaf kit
Clear acrylic spray sealer
Rubber cement
Pencil, ruler, T-square, craft knife
Flat paintbrush

DIRECTIONS

1. Use a T-square to mark a 14¼" x 6¾"
rectangle on illustration board.

2. Cut out rectangle using a craft knife
and ruler.

3. Mark two lines crosswise along rectangle, 4¾" from each short edge (sides).
Lightly score along these lines, following
General Directions on page 95, then fold
end panels of triptych in toward center.
Unfold, leaving end panels on a slight inward angle.

4. Give three coats of black enamel paint
to all surfaces of triptych, letting dry between coats.

5. Adhere gold tape around each panel of
triptych, ½" from edges, then again ⅛"
from edges. Between strips, lay ¼" strips
of gold leaf. Using a dry ballpoint pen or
small knitting needle and applying even
pressure, draw scrolls and curlicues over
gold leaf strips. Refer to actual-size diagram, but work freehand in the same
general pattern around each panel. Remove gold leaf strips.

6. Spray triptych with two light coats of
clear acrylic sealer.

7. From posterboard, cut three mats each
3½" x 5½". Mark a 2" x 4" window centered on mat, leaving a ¾" frame all
around. Using craft knife and ruler, cut
out window on *two* of the mats. On the
third, divide window crosswise in half
with a ½" bar, creating two smaller windows in a vertical row. Cut out the two
windows.

8. Strengthen giftwrap, following General Directions. Place each mat on wrong
side of giftwrap and trace around outsides and window openings. Cut out ½"
beyond outline. On each window, cut
diagonally from corner to corner. Dry-
mount giftwrap to mat, following General Directions. Bring edges of giftwrap
to wrong side, trimming away excess at
window openings.

9. Optional: Add gold leaf dots and
scrolls to mat fronts.

10. Cut clear acetate or plastic slightly
smaller all around than mats. Using rubber cement, glue to back of mats. Glue
each mat to a panel of triptych; place the
mat with two window openings in the
middle. Center each mat inside gold tape
and scrollwork designs, and glue only
along three edges, leaving one edge open
for inserting snapshots.

Actual-Size Diagram for Triptych
Picture Frame Scrollwork

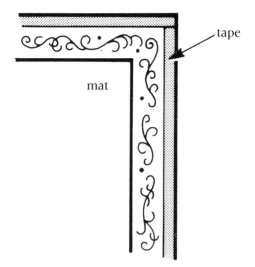

tape

mat

Tasseled Round Box

Giftwraps by Artists: Kimono: Japanese
 Designs
Round, lidded chipwood box
Clear acrylic spray sealer
Spray adhesive
Drill with ⅛″ bit
*Small upholstery tassel or 4″ of upholstery
 fringe plus embroidery floss in a
 matching color*
*Flat pendant or bauble (I used an enameled
 fan-shape earring minus its finding)*

DIRECTIONS
1. Strengthen giftwrap, following General Directions on page 95.
2. Cut pieces from giftwrap, using the chipwood box for patterns: Trace around top of lid and bottom of box twice. Cut out ¹⁄₁₆″ smaller all around.
3. Measure the height (H) and circumference (C) of box and lid. Cut rectangles from giftwrap, measuring C + ½″ in length, and the following widths: *For the box, H + ½″. For the box lining, H + ¼″. For the lid, 2H + ½″.*
4. Dry-mount giftwrap to box, following General Directions. *First, cover sides of box*: Center largest giftwrap rectangle in place. Overlap short edges. Bring top edge to inside of box. Bring bottom edge to underside of box, cutting into excess at regular intervals to create tabs. Tabs enable the giftwrap to hug the curve and prevent bulkiness. Adhere one circle to bottom of box.

Line inside of box: Cut ¼″ tabs into one long edge of next largest giftwrap rectangle. Adhere to inside of box so tabs extend onto bottom of box and short sides overlap. Adhere second circle inside bottom of box.

For lid: Before spraying giftwrap with adhesive, fold rectangle lengthwise in half, wrong sides facing, crease and unfold. Cut ¼″ tabs along both long edges of giftwrap rectangle. Spray with adhesive. Adhere to sides of lid, with crease along bottom edge of lid, short edges overlapping, and tabs brought to top and inside of lid. Glue a circle to the top of lid and another to the underside.

5. Lightly spray box and lid separately with two coats of acrylic sealer, letting dry after each coat.

6. Drill a hole in the center of the lid. If desired, follow directions for Stationery Holder to make a tassel with upholstery fringe. Thread a pendant or bauble onto the tassel string, and make a double knot. Thread string through hole and knot at underside of lid. Place a strip of tape across knot to secure.

PERSONALIZED STATIONERY

Party Time

Place Cards or Gift Tags
Napkin Cones
Pretty Chicken Centerpiece
Elegant Lunch Bags
Chinese Food Cartons
Christmas Tree Ornament Box

For me, one of the most rewarding moments before guests arrive at my home is when I take time for a last appraising look at the dining table: The silver is polished, the china and glassware are gleaming, the napkins are in place, and the centerpiece creates a festive focal point. The inspiration for the Pretty Chicken Centerpiece was a pattern I once saw on a piece of English bone china. I simply painted a purchased papier-mâché chicken and applied single blossoms over the entire body. Next, I connected the flowers by painting freehand the tendrils and leaves. Though the photograph does not show it, there is a cylinder-shaped cavity into which you can place a juice glass filled with flowers.

For less formal entertaining, but no less ceremonial a feast, I created the Elegant Lunch Bags. I planned a delicious meal that you can serve right out of carry bags made from giftwrap. Each course can be served or eaten directly from the plastic containers or Chinese take-out cartons, covered in coordinating giftwrap. Add plastic utensils and matching paper napkins and you are all set. The scrumptious lunch shown here was prepared by Jonathan Randall of Jonathan's, Huntington, New York.

A simple way to safeguard and store precious Christmas tree ornaments is to partition a box, making snug compartments for each ornament. The holidays are a busy time and having your ornament collection organized in a pretty box will bring pleasure and peace of mind.

Place Cards or Gift Tags

MATERIALS
Giftwraps by Artists: English Floral
  Patterns
Heavy white paper
Craft knife
Spray adhesive
Fine green felt-tip marking pen

DIRECTIONS
1. Cut 3½" x 4½" rectangles from heavy white paper. If desired, score along crosswise center and fold.
2. Cut out small motifs from giftwrap.
3. Apply adhesive spray to wrong side of motifs. Let set for a minute or two, then press to left half of card.
4. Draw a graceful tendril: a series of small curlicues, from motif across bottom of card.
5. For place card, write each guest's name above the tendril. For a gift tag, write the recipient's name on the outside or inside of the card.

Napkin Cones

MATERIALS
Giftwraps by Artists: English Floral
  Patterns
Cardboard
White cotton fabric strip 1¾" x 20"
Rubber cement
Découpage medium
Glue gun and hot-melt glue sticks

Watercolor paints: lime green and emerald
Large sheet of white paper
Pencil, ruler
Compass
Scissors
Spring-type clothespin
Cellophane wrap
Tapered paintbrush

DIRECTIONS
1. Make pattern: On white paper, use compass to scribe a circle with a 6⅝" radius. Fold circle into quarters and cut out one quarter-circle wedge.
2. Place pattern on cardboard and trace around. Cut out.
3. Select giftwrap and strengthen, following General Directions on page 95.
4. Place pattern on wrong side of giftwrap and trace around twice. Cut out first wedge along marked line (lining), second wedge ½" beyond marked line.
5. Following General Directions, dry-mount lining to wrong side of cardboard wedge.
6. Wrap cardboard wedge into a cone, with lining inside and straight edges overlapping by ⅜". Hot-glue straight edges together.
7. Fold straight edges of remaining giftwrap wedge ⅛" to wrong side. Glue with rubber cement. Following General Directions, dry-mount this wedge around the cardboard cone, overlapping straight edges. Giftwrap will extend beyond rim of cone; clip into excess at ½" intervals and fold over rim onto inside of cone.
8. Dip fabric strip into découpage medium. While still wet, fashion a bow as follows: Turn long edges ¼" to wrong side, and cut a 7½", a 9½", and a 3" length. Bring ends of the 7½" length together

and overlap, forming a ring. Flatten ring slightly with the overlap at center. Place on center of 9½" length. Wrap both tightly with remaining short length, for "bow knot". Place on cellophane wrap and secure at center with clothespin. For each streamer, turn end ½" to wrong side, and make a loop at center, bringing streamer ends in closely. Let dry.

9. Cut tiny flowers and leaves from giftwrap and découpage along bow, following General Directions.

10. Freehand, paint small leaves and stems along bow, filling spaces between découpaged motifs. Let dry, then seal with another coat of découpage medium.

11. Hot-glue bow to rim of cone.

Pretty Chicken Centerpiece

MATERIALS

Giftwraps by Artists: English Floral
    Patterns
*Purchased papier-mâché figurine; my hen
    with a well for a potted plant is from
    Palechek (write to them at P.O. Box 225,
    Richmond, California 94808, for store
    nearest you)*
*High-gloss enamel paint in white or desired
    background color*
Lime and emerald green acrylic paints
High-gloss découpage medium
Fine, tapered paintbrush
Flat, 1" paintbrush

DIRECTIONS

1. Paint all surfaces of figurine with two light coats of high-gloss paint, letting dry and sanding if necessary after each coat.

2. Choose a giftwrap with a floral motif and strengthen giftwrap, following General Directions on page 95.

3. Cut out motifs, omitting fine, lined stems. Découpage all around papier-mâché figure, following General Directions. Begin with largest motifs, and space them out randomly over figurine. Turn them in various positions to achieve variety and a sense of movement. Place medium-sized and small motifs in between; avoid overlapping shapes. Finally, découpage small leaves or leaf clusters in any remaining open spaces.

4. Using lime green paint and fine, tapered paintbrush, work freehand to add gracefully curvy vines, stems and leaves. Fill in any remaining spaces, link separate motifs, tie individual leaves in to adjacent sprigs, and continue design into places less accessible for découpage.

5. Using emerald green paint, add detail and emphasis: Create a prominent leaf shape at eye position. Add a stroke of shading or fine veins to lime green leaves. Correct any miscut motifs or abrupt outlines with a small painted leaf or stem. Let dry.

6. Coat with several light applications of découpage medium, until surface is shiny and thoroughly smooth.

58

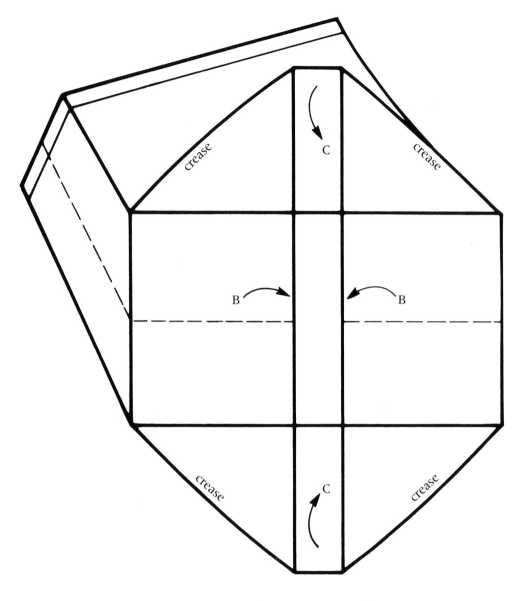

Figure 2: Bottom of Bag

Elegant Lunch Bags

MATERIALS

Giftwraps by Artists: Vienna Style
1 yard clear self-adhesive plastic
Rubber cement
Cardboard
Hole punch
¾ yard twisted satin cord, ¼" thick

DIRECTIONS

1. Select and strengthen one sheet of giftwrap, following General Directions on page 95.
2. Spread giftwrap flat on a tabletop, wrong side up. Using sharp pencil and ruler, lightly mark off solid and dashed lines as shown in Fig. 1. (*Note:* For the taller bags shown, increase the height of the bag sides by 2".) Cut out complete rectangle along outside lines.
3. Following General Directions, laminate rectangle with self-adhesive plastic.
4. Make fold lines along all marked lines, folding *up* along solid lines, *back* along dash lines. Crease all folds, then unfold.
5. Place rubber cement along areas marked A on diagram, on wrong side. Bring short edges of rectangle together, overlapping A areas with right edge. Smooth, press, and let glue set.
6. Fold B areas toward center as shown in Fig. 2. Match straight side lines of each B area to a top line of adjacent C area. This forms each C area into a triangle (with a somewhat truncated tip). Apply rubber cement to bottom corners of triangle between layers; crease along sides of triangle as shown in Fig. 2.

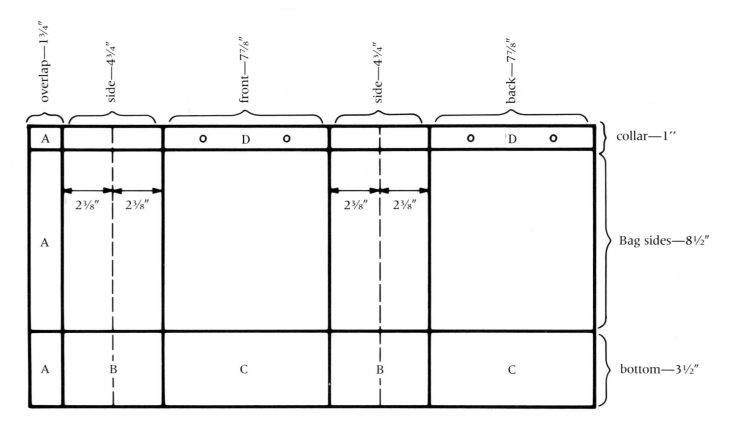

Figure 1: Marking Diagram for Elegant Lunch Bags

7. Fold first one C triangle, then the other C triangle toward the center. Rubber cement them to B sections and to each other to secure. Place a small weight, such as a bag of dried beans, in the bottom of bag until glue dries.

8. From cardboard, cut two rectangles ⅞" x 7¾". Glue one to wrong side of each D area. Gently fold the top of bag 1" to inside all around. Recrease all folds around top of bag. Apply glue around the top of bag between layers and press to secure. Let dry.

9. On each D area, punch a hole 1½" from each short end, through all layers. Cut twisted satin cord in half. On the

front of the bag, insert ends of one cord through punched holes, from the outside of the bag to the inside. Dab ends with rubber cement and make a tight knot; trim beyond knot. Repeat on the back of the bag.

10. To strengthen the bottom of bag, make a base: Cut a 4⅝" x 7¾" rectangle from cardboard. Cover with giftwrap, then with self-adhesive plastic, using rubber cement as necessary. Place in the bottom of the bag.

11. To fold the bag flat, bring the sides in along dash lines. Bring front and back of bag together as close to bottom as possible. Fold bag back on its bottom; crease.

Chinese Food Cartons

NOTE
Carton is best used with wrapped or dry contents, as finished carton may be wiped but not washed.

MATERIALS
Giftwraps by Artists: Vienna Style
Clean, unused cartons from a Chinese take-out restaurant
Clear acrylic spray
Adhesive spray
Pliers
Craft knife
Tapestry needle

DIRECTIONS
1. Select giftwrap: one pattern for entire carton, or one for the exterior, a complementary pattern for the interior. Strengthen giftwrap, following General Directions on page 95.
2. Using pliers, open up hooks and remove wire handles from carton. Open carton out and flatten.
3. Following General Directions, dry-mount carton to giftwrap, using adhesive spray. Smooth from the giftwrap side. Let dry. Place on a protected surface, carton side up, and cut giftwrap with a craft knife following the edges of the carton. Also cut the slit along one top flap and pierce holes for the wire through the giftwrap.
4. Repeat Step 3, dry-mounting the same or a complementary pattern to the reverse side of the carton.

5. Refold carton as before, and reinstall wire handle; *or* for a simpler, more elegant exterior, bring side flaps to inside of box and secure with tape or glue. Pierce sides with a needle, then insert ends of wire handle; pinch ends with pliers to secure.

Christmas Tree Ornament Box

MATERIALS
Giftwraps by Artists: American Quilts
Illustration board
1 yard self-adhesive plastic
Cardboard
¼ yard dark green pin-dot fabric
Glue gun and hot-melt glue sticks
Rubber cement
Découpage medium
Pencil, ruler
Scissors, craft knife
Spring-type clothespin
Cellophane wrap

DIRECTIONS
1. Following Fig. 1, mark the box on illustration board. Using a ruler and craft knife and working on a protected surface, cut out along outlines. Score along dash lines; see General Directions on page 95 for scoring instructions.
2. Bring up sides of box, perpendicular to bottom. Hot-glue sides of box together.
3. Following General Directions, laminate giftwrap with self-adhesive plastic. Cut out the following rectangles: 13" x 18", 2" x 17½", and 6¼" x 7".

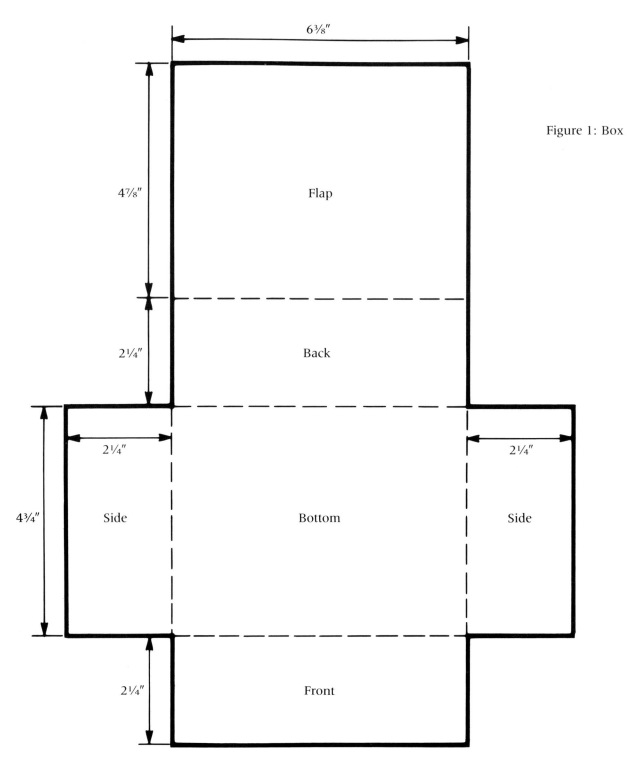

6⅜″

4⅞″

Flap

2¼″

Back

2¼″

Side

4¾″

Side

2¼″

Bottom

2¼″

Front

2¼″

Figure 1: Box

Christmas Tree Ornament Box

4. Following General Directions, dry-mount the largest rectangle around box: Begin by centering one 13" edge on inside front edge of box. Wrap all around, over flap, bringing opposite 13" edge inside flap. Bring up side edges, cutting at the corners so giftwrap lies flat, and secure inside box. Dry-mount the 2" strip inside box around sides and front. Dry-mount the remaining rectangle to the inside surface of the flap and back of box, centering carefully.

5. Cut fabric into 2¼"-wide strips. Dip into découpage medium. While still wet, turn long edges ¼" to wrong side and finger-press. Cut one 25" length and adhere to box centered between side edges: Begin at bottom of box on the inside, place along inside of back, inside flap, outside flap, outside back, bottom, front, inside front, and onto bottom. Secure with bits of masking tape until dry.

6. With remainder of wet fabric strip, fashion a bow: Cut a 12", 4", and two 7½" lengths. Bring ends of the 12" length together and overlap, forming a ring. Flatten ring slightly with overlap at center. Wrap center tightly with the 4" length, for a bowknot. Place on box at the beginning of the flap. Secure bowknot with a clothespin. For streamers, place end of each 7½" length under bowknot, extending diagonally to the left and right. Turn ends ½" to the wrong side, and make little loops along streamers, to "scrunch" them closely. Let dry.

7. Box insert: Cut an 8" x 14" rectangle from cardboard. Round corners slightly. Following General Directions, dry-mount giftwrap to right side. Following Fig. 2 and using pencil and ruler, mark all dimensions for insert on wrong side of cardboard. Using a craft knife and ruler, cut out along heavy outlines, and score where indicated by fine lines. Turn to right side, and following diagram, score where indicated by short dash lines. Pinch A to B. Pinch each C to the adjacent D. This forms six sections. Place the insert in the box.

Figure 2: Box Insert

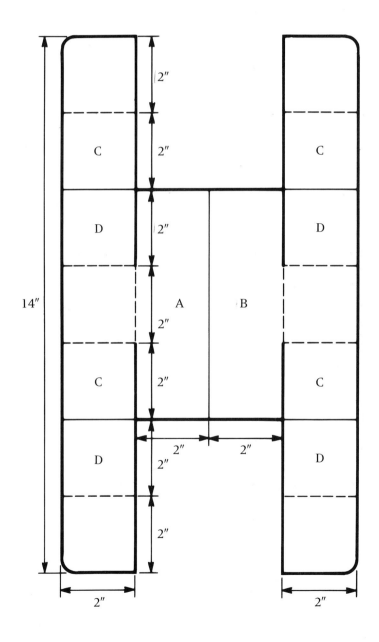

GIFTS

Baby Basket

Octagonal Picture Frame
Baby Album
Pamper Hamper
Framed Birth Announcement

The Baby Gift Basket includes items that relate to the new baby: a Framed Birth Announcement, an Octagonal Picture Frame, a Baby Album, and a Hamper for disposable diapers. The basket is large enough to serve as a portable bassinet for a newborn (and perfect for filling with gifts before the event). You may wish to include in the Octagonal Picture Frame a picture of the mother-to-be when she herself was a baby. Leave the second space blank to be filled in by the mother as she wishes. It would be quite lovely to see the baby's first photo in the second spot. Another ideal place for photos and special memories is the Baby Album, a keepsake that can serve as a journal of the mother's pregnancy as well as a record of the baby's first year. You may wish to create decorative containers using the giftwraps that coordinate with the nursery. The Framed Birth Announcement can be made ahead of time and filled in at baby's birth; or, you may wish to adapt the idea in principle and commemorate Mother's Day instead. The Pamper Hamper is a little more complicated to construct but well worth the effort; giftwrap from the *American Quilt* collection lines the interior of the Hamper, but you can cover the outside in giftwrap as well. In addition, you may wish to create a variety of albums for baby and family such as "Baby's First Christmas," "Baby's First Birthday," etc. If you make one book each year, you will have lovely keepsakes to present to the child later on in life, perhaps on the occasion of marriage.

Octagonal Picture Frame

MATERIALS

Giftwraps by Artists: Art Nouveau *and* English Floral Patterns
Double-weight illustration board
Artist's or flint paper in two contrasting colors and textures
Heavy clear-plastic sheet
⅝ yard clear self-adhesive plastic
Rubber cement
Pencil, ruler
Craft knife, scissors
Stapler and staples
Crayon, grease pencil, or permanent ink felt-tip marking pen

DIRECTIONS

1. Mark a 9⅝" x 7⅝" rectangle on illustration board. Mark points, 1⅝" from each corner on each side. Connect points across each corner, forming an octagon. Use craft knife and ruler to cut out octagon, for frame back. Trace onto illustration board and cut out a second octagon, for frame front. On one octagon, mark lines 1½" inside outline. Cut out, for a window opening.

2. Place frame front on each sheet of art paper and trace around outside and window opening. Cut both sheets ¼" smaller all around. On one, mark lines ⅜" to the inside of the window opening. Cut out, using a craft knife and ruler.

3. Select giftwrap and laminate with clear self-adhesive plastic, following General Directions on page 95.

4. Place frame front and frame back on wrong side of plastic-coated giftwrap. Trace around pieces. Cut out 1" larger all around, and 1" to the inside of the window opening. Cut up to marked line at each angle. Following General Directions, dry-mount illustration board to wrong side of giftwrap; wrap giftwrap edges to back of board.

5. *Easel stand:* Cut a 2" x 7¾" strip of illustration board. Dry-mount giftwrap over both sides, then cover with clear self-adhesive plastic. Place one short edge at the center of one long edge of frame back; staple 1" and 1¼" from edge. Bend easel stand back slightly.

6. Using rubber cement, glue background to frame back, wrong sides together. Glue mat on top. Cut two snapshots into 1¾" x 2½" ovals. Glue to background, centering side by side within mat. From floral giftwrap, cut out a sprig of flowers around 4½" in length. Apply rubber cement sparingly to back, then glue across tops of snapshot ovals.

7. Place frame front on clear-plastic sheet and trace around with crayon, grease pencil, or felt-tip marker. Cut out ¼" to inside of marked line. Glue plastic to back of frame front.

8. Glue frame front to frame back, with background and mat in between.

Baby Album

MATERIALS

Giftwraps by Artists: English Floral Patterns
Matboard
Two 9" squares of cotton calico fabric
Small carved goose with bow, 3¼" tall (Classic Carvings #8616, available at Leewards or write Kittay & Blitz, Inc., 12 Industrial Lane, Johnston, Rhode Island 02919, for store nearest you)
White high-gloss enamel paint
Acrylic paints: white, robin's egg blue, golden yellow, light green, gray
Pad of charcoal paper in various colors
White quilting thread
¼ yard muslin craft ribbon 1¼" wide
1¼ yards moss green grosgrain ribbon ⅜" wide
Spray adhesive
Découpage medium
Rubber cement
Pencil, ruler, T-square
Craft knife, scissors
Glue gun and hot-melt glue sticks
Flat and fine, tapered paintbrushes
Sharp tapestry needle

DIRECTIONS

1. Using pencil and ruler, mark a 15½" x 7¾" rectangle on charcoal paper. Cut out, using a craft knife and ruler. Place rectangle on 3 other sheets and cut out with craft knife and ruler. Stack 4 sheets together, then fold crosswise in half, to form a "folio". Make 4 folios in this manner.

2. Thread tapestry needle with quilting thread; knot close to end. Unfold each

folio, and insert needle through pages on fold line, 2″ from bottom edge. Make three long (¾″) running stitches up the fold line, then knot thread close to surface.

3. Refold folios and stack, with cut and folded edges even. Trim muslin craft ribbon to a 7¾″ length. Apply rubber cement to outside folds of folios. Center along length of muslin ribbon, keeping long edges of ribbon free. Let dry.

4. Use pencil, ruler, and T-square to mark the following rectangles on matboard, then cut them out, using ruler and craft knife: one 8″ x 17⅛″, one 8″ x 8½″, two 7¾″ squares, one ½″ x 24″, one ½″ x 10″.

5. Dry-mount one calico fabric square to one side of each 7¾″ matboard square; follow General Directions on page 95 and use spray adhesive. Begin by centering matboard on fabric. Bring corners to wrong side. Fold in sides, using rubber cement to secure neatly at corners.

6. Score remaining matboard rectangles, following General Directions: Place largest matboard rectangle on work surface with short edges at the sides; score a parallel, vertical line 8″ from each short edge. On 8″ x 8½″ rectangle, score a line ½″ from one short edge, dividing rectangle into an 8″ square (front cover) and a ½″ x 8″ binding. Score the ½″ x 24″ strip at 8″ intervals. Fold all pieces at right angles along scorings.

7. Give matboard pieces and goose figurine 2 light coats of white enamel paint—one side only. Let dry thoroughly after each coat.

8. Transfer outline only for oval pattern to center of front cover. Carefully cut out with craft knife.

9. Assemble cover with hot-glue gun as follows, keeping matboard pieces perpendicular to each other, and front surfaces flush: First, hot-glue smallest strip around oval cutout. Trim short ends so they butt, and hot-glue to join. Hot-glue ½″ x 24″ strip around top, right side, and bottom edges of front cover. Hot-glue short edges of this strip to short edges of binding. This completes the 3-D front cover. Apply rubber cement to back edges of strip wrapped around the oval cutout. Hot-glue 3-D front cover to right side of largest rectangle.

10. Touch up with white paint along matboard edges and for ½″ along inside edges of cover.

11. Paint back surface of oval, referring to pattern: Paint top two-thirds with blue paint, then immediately smudge white paint in a circular motion to create clouds. Paint lower third of oval green, quickly adding a little gray to create trees on the horizon, and grassy texture in the foreground.

12. For goose, paint beak and feet yellow. Paint bow blue. Paint a gray eye.

13. Découpage around oval cutout, following General Directions for technique. From floral giftwrap, cut four similar sprigs or bouquets. Staying ¼″ from oval edges, apply slightly larger bouquets at bottom corners, remaining bouquets at top corners. Before applying coats of découpage medium, use a fine, tapered paintbrush and pale green paint to add stems, leaves, and tendrils, to soften and link bouquets.

14. Apply several light coats of découpage medium to entire front cover, including oval area, and, separately, to goose figurine.

15. Using rubber cement, adhere goose to center of oval.

16. Cut ⅜″ yard grosgrain ribbon. Hot-glue end of ribbon to inside of binding.

17. Apply rubber cement to muslin craft ribbon which binds the folios. Adhere to the inside of the album binding, covering the ribbon end.

18. Use rubber cement to glue fabric-covered squares to inside covers.

19. Cut remainder of grosgrain ribbon into 8″ lengths. Use to cover outside surface of binding, gluing side by side with rubber cement. Apply découpage medium on top to seal binding.

Actual-Size Pattern for Baby Album Front Cover Oval

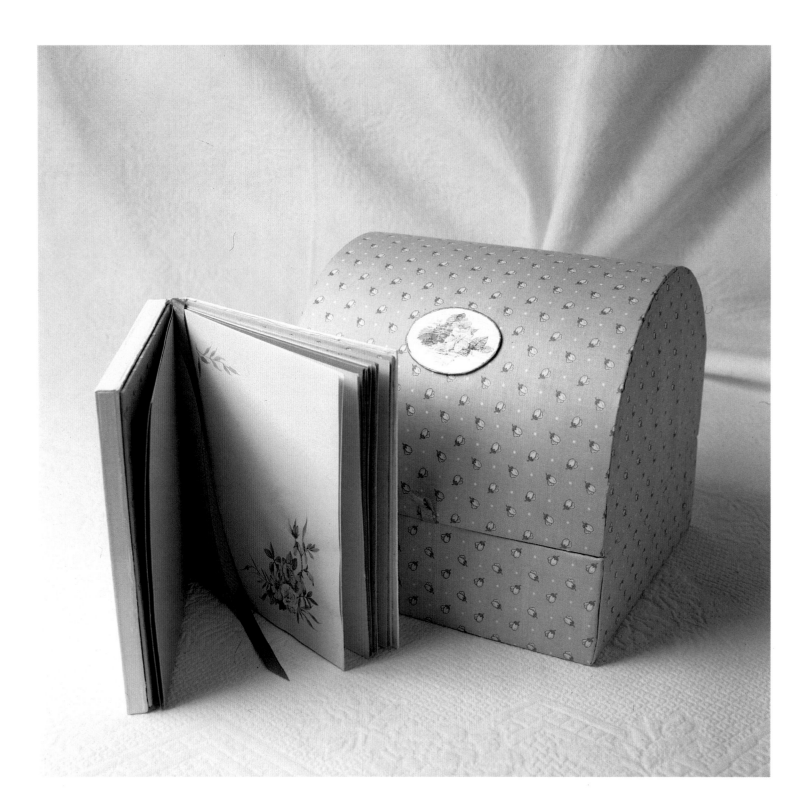

Pamper Hamper

MATERIALS

Giftwraps by Artists: American Quilts *and* English Floral Patterns
1 yard cotton calico fabric 44" wide
Matboard
1 yard clear self-adhesive plastic
½ yard feather-edge grosgrain ribbon ⅜" wide, in color to match fabric
Permanent ink felt-tip pen in color to contrast with fabric

Spray adhesive
Rubber cement
Compass
Pencil, ruler, T-square
Craft knife, scissors for cutting fabric and paper
Glue gun and hot-melt glue sticks
Carbon or graphite paper

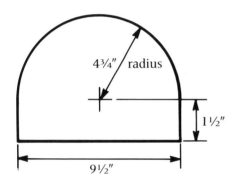

Diagram for Pamper Hamper Lid Sides

4¾" radius

1½"

9½"

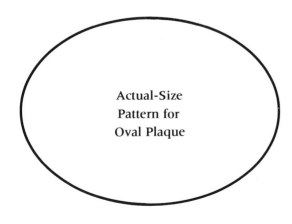

Actual-Size
Pattern for
Oval Plaque

DIRECTIONS

1. On matboard, mark the following pieces, using a compass, T-square, and pencil: for barrel lid, a 9½" x 18¼" rectangle; for each of two lid sides, a semicircle with 4¾" radius combined with a 9½" x 1½" rectangle along its straight side (see diagram); for box bottom, a 9½" square; for box sides, a 3" x 38" rectangle.

2. Cut out all pieces with a craft knife, using a ruler for all straight edges.

3. Laminate giftwrap, to be used for lining hamper, with clear self-adhesive plastic, following General Directions on page 95.

4. Place matboard pieces for barrel lid and lid sides on wrong side of laminated giftwrap and trace around. Cut out giftwrap along marker lines with the following exceptions: for barrel lid, cut out ¼" smaller along short ends, ½" larger along long edges; for barrel sides, cut out ¼" smaller along long straight edge. Mark the following pieces on wrong side of laminated giftwrap, using a T-square and pencil: for box back/bottom/front: a 10" x 15" rectangle; for sides, two 2¾" x 9½" rectangles. Set lining pieces aside.

Note: You may wish to cover the exterior as well as the interior of the Pamper Hamper with laminated giftwrap. If so,

follow Steps 5, 7, and 8, substituting laminated giftwrap whenever fabric is indicated.

5. Place barrel lid and lid sides on wrong side of fabric, 1" apart with straight edges along the grain. Trace around each piece with pencil. Remove matboard pieces. Cut out fabric, cutting ½" beyond all straight lines, and ⅛" to the *inside* of curved lines.

6. Assemble lid: hot-glue one long edge of barrel lid around curved edge of lid side. Repeat on other long edge of barrel lid.

7. Spray adhesive on wrong side of fabric for barrel lid. Center on corresponding matboard piece. Press smoothly into place. Wrap excess fabric along short ends (front and back of hamper) to underside of lid. Cut ½" tabs at ½" intervals into fabric which extends over curved side edges; press down onto sides. Spray adhesive on wrong side of fabric for lid sides. Center on each side, ⅛" from curved edges, and bring straight bottom edge tautly to the underside.

8. Cut a 17½" square of fabric. Spray wrong side with adhesive, and center bottom of box on top. Bring fabric up over two opposite sides (front and back of hamper), and adhere edges to inside surfaces. Bring fabric up over sides of hamper, making neat "hospital corners" and securing them with rubber cement.

9. Position lid so its back edge touches the back of the box, with lid and box at right angles to one another. Place books or other props under and behind lid to keep it in this position. Make a hinge: From fabric, cut out a 2½" x 9" rectangle. Fold it lengthwise in half, wrong sides facing, and crease. Using rubber cement,

glue it along the inside back edges: half to the barrel lid, half to the box.

10. Cut two 6″ strands of ribbon. Apply hot glue to the end of one strand and press to lid side, 3″ from back corner; stretch ribbon down to corresponding box side, 3″ from back corner, and hot-glue other end to inside of box. Repeat on other side of box with second strand of ribbon. These ribbons will support the lid and prevent it from falling all the way back when the hamper is opened.

11. Fold remaining ribbon in half. Using hot glue, adhere 1½″ ends to inside of barrel lid at center front. Bring loop up to right side and glue for ½″.

12. Clip up to marked lines on barrel lid lining, to make ¼″ tabs at ½″ intervals.

13. Following General Directions and using rubber cement, dry-mount lining pieces to inside of box as follows: Center barrel lid lining in place, bringing tabs down onto curved lid sides. Adhere lid sides in place. Center box back/bottom/front inside box; crease it into the corners. Clip into the excess at the corners and bring the edges ¼″ up onto the sides. Dry-mount one of the smaller lining rectangles in place at each side.

14. Plaque: Transfer actual-size pattern for oval plaque onto matboard, using carbon or graphite paper. Cut out smoothly along outline. Mark along edges for ⅛″ with permanent ink felt-tip pen. Cut out a small floral motif from giftwrap. Following General Directions, découpage to plaque. Using rubber cement, glue oval to center front of barrel lid, as shown.

Framed Birth Announcement

MATERIALS

Giftwraps by Artists: English Floral Patterns
Flint paper in coordinating color
White acrylic or oil paint, thinned
Tacky craft glue
Pencil, ruler
Tracing paper
Dressmaker's tracing (carbon) paper in white or a light color
Craft knife, small sharp scissors
Paper clips
Fine, tapered paintbrush
Wood toothpick
9″ x 12″ frame with glass

DIRECTIONS

1. Select desired giftwrap and strengthen, following General Directions on page 95.

2. Using pencil and ruler, mark a 9″ x 12″ rectangle on giftwrap, or dimensions to fit frame. Cut out, for mat.

3. Using pencil and ruler, lightly mark window opening: a 6″ x 9″ rectangle centered on mat. Mark a ½″ diagonal line across each corner and erase previous corner markings.

4. To create "filigree" in window opening: Place mat on a protected surface. Using a craft knife, cut away background only within marked lines for window opening, leaving desired vines, tendrils, and flowers. If desired, work closely around motifs with small scissors. If you are not left with a few empty areas for placing lettering, particularly in a central area, remove some of the motifs.

5. Place mat on flint paper and trace around outer edge. Secure the two layers together temporarily with paper clips.

6. Place a sheet of tracing paper over mat and flint paper. Lightly pencil the outlines of the window opening, then write the text of your announcement within the empty spaces. Use a simple script; if desired, add an extra curlicue or flourish to beginning letters, a graceful swash to ending letters. Place name(s) of the person in the center, or largest space, then fill other spaces with documentary information. For example, in the birth announcement pictured, the first name of the child, written in large script, occupies the center space. Directly above the name: "Announcing the birth of," with a date below the name. In other spaces, time of birth, weight of baby, and parents' names are recorded.

7. When pleased with your arrangement of text, insert a sheet of dressmaker's carbon paper, ink side down. Lightly go over all lettering to transfer it to the flint paper. Remove tracing paper, carbon paper, and mat.

8. Using a fine paintbrush and thin white paint, go over all text. Let dry.

9. Turn mat to reverse side. Using a wood pick, dot craft glue onto back of each motif. Use glue sparingly. Also apply glue around window opening. Place mat over flint paper, matching up outer edges of mat with penciled line of flint paper. Let dry.

10. Cut out flint paper to match outside edge of mat. Insert behind glass into frame.

GIFTS

Wedding Basket

Picnic Hamper
Looseleaf Notebook and
   Folding File with Slipcase
Vase Sleeve
"Our Wedding" Album

Decorated with a spray of silk flowers and bouquets cut from *English Floral Patterns,* this white Picnic Hamper holds the ingredients of a honeymoon breakfast. When planning the gifts for the bride and groom, consider making the two-volume record-keeping book in the slipcase. These volumes, a covered Looseleaf Notebook and an expanding Folding File, can help the newlyweds organize their household records; these same elements can be used to form a recipe and menu file, or a vacation file. For the bridal shower you can make the beautiful Wedding Album and the matching Vase Sleeve for the flower vase.

Picnic Hamper

MATERIALS

Giftwraps by Artists: English Floral
    Patterns
*Small picnic basket with hamper lid and
    handles*
*Glossy white enamel paint (in pint or spray
    can)*
Découpage medium
Leaf green or olive green paint
Clear acrylic spray sealer
*Stem of small white silk flowers, such as
    lily-of-the-valley*
⅜ yard blue grosgrain ribbon ⅛" wide
Glue gun and hot-melt glue sticks
Broad flat, and fine tapered paintbrushes

DIRECTIONS

1. Paint entire basket, inside and out, with glossy white paint, using broad, flat brush or spray can. Let dry thoroughly. Repeat for a total of three to four coats.
2. Select a giftwrap containing several desirable floral sprigs; follow General Directions on page 95 to strengthen giftwrap.
3. Cut out several sprigs of flowers, including leaves and stems. Découpage cutouts as follows, following General Directions; be sure to press down the tiny snippets of giftwrap motifs until they adhere. First, apply a few flowers in a graceful curve over top front of basket. Open hamper lid and create a design on the interior side. Apply several floral sprigs to the center of the lid, with motifs radiating outward (like the spokes of a wheel) in all directions except for straight down.
4. With a fine tapered paintbrush, and green paint, continue stems of all sprigs on lid from the center straight down, as if flowers were all being gathered into a bouquet.
5. Apply at least two light coats of découpage medium or clear acrylic spray over both design areas.
6. Tie ribbon into a simple bow. Hot-glue bowknot to top of painted stems. Hot-glue each streamer at three different points, looping and curving the ribbon in between.
7. Cut stem of silk flowers apart into several small sprigs. Hot-glue over découpaged flowers for added depth.

Looseleaf Notebook and Folding File with Slipcase

MATERIALS

Giftwraps by Artists: William Morris
    (Note: *you will need 3 identical sheets for
    the set as shown. To economize,
    substitute a different, complementary
    sheet for each project.*)
2½ yards clear self-adhesive plastic
*Purchased small looseleaf notebook,
    7½" x 10"*
Purchased folding file, 9½" x 7½"
Double-weight illustration board
Tagboard in color to match giftwrap
White acrylic paint
*Permanent ink fine black felt-tip marking
    pen*
1¼ yards white lace or loop trim
⅝ yard white satin ribbon, ⅜" wide
Glue gun and hot-melt glue sticks
Rubber cement
Pencil, ruler
Craft knife, scissors
Small, tapered paintbrush

DIRECTIONS

1. Select giftwrap(s); see note above. Following General Directions on page 95, laminate giftwrap with clear self-adhesive plastic.
2. *Looseleaf Notebook:* Open out notebook flat on wrong side of laminated giftwrap. Trace around, and mark each corner of notebook spine. Cut out 1" beyond marked line. Clip up to markings at spine corners, then fold giftwrap 1" to wrong side between clippings; glue inside fold with rubber cement. Following General Directions, dry-mount giftwrap to front and back covers of looseleaf, wrapping edges to inside covers. With notebook closed, trace around front and back; cut out ¼" smaller all around. Dry-mount to inside covers, centering and staying well clear of looseleaf rings.
3. *Folding File:* Reinforce flap with double-weight illustration board, cut to same size and glued underneath with rubber cement. Open out flap and place file on wrong side of laminated giftwrap; trace around, marking the points on either side where the flap begins. Cut out 1" larger all around and clip up to marked points. Fold edges 1" to wrong side below clipped points, and glue inside folds with rubber cement. Following General Directions, dry-mount piece to back of file and exterior of flap, folding edges to interior of flap. Place flap on wrong side of giftwrap and trace around.

Cut out ½" longer on the bottom and ¼" smaller along all other edges, for lining. Dry-mount to flap interior, inserting the extra ½" behind the file. Trace front of file onto giftwrap and cut out; dry-mount in place.

4. *Slipcase:* (*Note:* Measurements which follow are based on stated sizes for notebook and file; if you are using different sizes, adjust the dimensions for the box accordingly.) From double-weight illustration board, cut the following rectangles: two 7½" x 10¼" (sides), two 3½" x 7½" (top and bottom), and one 3½" x 10¼" (spine). Hot-glue top, then bottom, over edges of sides, then hot-glue spine in back. Cut rectangles of laminated giftwrap: one 11" x 21", two 3⅛" x 8½". Following General Directions, dry-mount large rectangle over sides and spine, wrapping excess edges to inside and onto top and bottom. Cover top and bottom with smaller rectangles, wrapping excess to inside. If desired, cut a 2" x 27" strip of laminated giftwrap and dry-mount around the inside of box, close to the opening, for a partial lining.

5. *Spine Labels:* From tagboard, cut three rectangles 1½" x 2". Using pencil, neatly print label for each part of your set. In our set, we wrote "Budget & Directory" to label the notebook, "Bills" to label the file, and "HOME ORGANIZER" to label the slipcase. When satisfied with lettering, go over it with black felt-tip pen. Paint scrolls or decorative brackets in the corners of the labels. Glue lace trim around back of labels. Cut ribbon into 7" lengths. Fold each in half and glue ends behind label, so loop "pull" hangs straight down from bottom center. Glue labels to spines with rubber cement.

Vase Sleeve

MATERIALS
Giftwraps by Artists: English Floral
    Patterns
Oaktag
Clear self-adhesive plastic
Rubber cement
Glue gun and hot-melt glue stick
Pencil, ruler, tape measure
Craft knife, scissors
Jar, can, or inexpensive vase

DIRECTIONS
1. Cut oaktag to wrap around vase: Mark a rectangle with a width ½" greater than height of jar (can, or vase), and with a length 1" greater than circumference of jar. Cut out with a ruler and craft knife.
2. Select giftwrap and lay it wrong side up on your work surface. Place oaktag rectangle on top and trace around. Cut out giftwrap 1" larger all around. Cut out clear self-adhesive plastic to the same size.
3. Dry-mount giftwrap centered over oaktag, following General Directions on page 95. Bring excess edges of giftwrap to wrong side of oaktag.
4. Bring short edges of giftwrap/oaktag rectangle together to form a cylindrical "sleeve" for the jar. Overlap edges by ½" and hot-glue to secure.
5. Wrap clear self-adhesive plastic all around sleeve, overlapping short edges and bringing excess plastic to the inside at top and bottom.
6. Fill jar with water and carefully slip the sleeve over it. Arrange flowers.

"Our Wedding" Album

(See page 38 for instructions)

GIFTS

His Basket

Accordion Recipe File
Paisley ''Wine Labels'' Book

The idea of giving *him* a basket of *anything* never occurred to me until I realized the vast promise such an idea held when filled with gifts related to *his* interest or hobby. When preparing the His Basket, I went straight to an expert, Jonathan Randall of Jonathan's in Huntington, New York. Because my husband, John, loves to cook (and I do not), I needed some guidance in preparing a basket filled with gourmet cooking ingredients for the experienced cook, the kind of ingredients that one does not usually have on hand. Here is what Jonathan suggested: porcini mushrooms, raspberry vinegar, fresh shallots, fresh herbs, coffee beans, olive oil, and imported mustard. You can begin a file of recipes, using an expanding file; you can add some great wines along with the handmade book for wine labels. If your ''his'' is a baker, there is a plethora of possibilities. Another possibility is to create a gift basket around a gardening theme; create a slipcase for a favorite gardening book or create a garden diary for recording his planting schedule. Search through *English Floral Patterns* for blooms that may relate to your garden; trace patterns from business envelopes onto the giftwrap to make storage envelopes for seeds.

Paisley "Wine Labels" Book

(see page 23 for instructions).

Accordion Recipe File

MATERIALS

Giftwraps by Artists: American Quilts
Purchased medium manila accordion file
Matboard
¾ yard clear self-adhesive plastic
Old print or engraving for label
Flat, broad felt-tip (calligraphy) pen
½ yard black silk cord
Rubber cement
Pencil, ruler
Craft knife

DIRECTIONS

1. Place accordion file flat on matboard; trace around.

2. Mark lines ⅛" beyond traced lines. Following actual-size diagram, mark "feet" along bottom edge at corners. Using a ruler and craft knife, cut out along outside marked lines.

3. Trace resulting shape onto matboard and cut out a second piece, for back.

4. Lay matboard shapes on the wrong side of giftwrap and trace around. Cut out giftwrap 1" larger all around.

5. Laminate giftwrap pieces with self-adhesive plastic.

6. Following General Directions on page 95, dry-mount giftwrap to matboard, centering carefully. Cut giftwrap up to matboard at corners and along curves. Using extra rubber cement, wrap edges of giftwrap to back of matboard.

7. Glue front and back centered onto accordion file, with feet extending at bottom.

8. From unlaminated giftwrap, cut two pieces slightly smaller all around than accordion file. Dry-mount each sheet inside front and back covers.

9. Find a small black-and-white print or engraving in an old book or magazine. Glue to front of file. Add a strip of paper in the same tone, and write "His," a name, or monogram in script, using the broad calligraphy pen.

10. Pierce a hole through front and back at the center. Pull one length of silk cord through each hold, knotting it on the inside to secure. Use to tie the file closed.

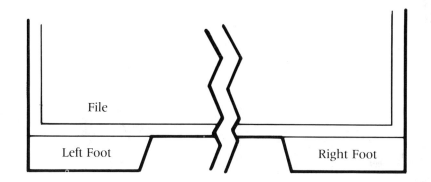

Actual-Size Diagram for Accordion File

GIFTS

For Children

Brother and Sister Paper Dolls
Dinosaurs

For Lovers and Friends

Love-Letter Trunk
Costume Jewelry

Children love working with their hands and will be inspired by the variety of patterns and colors available in all of the books in the *Giftwraps by Artists* series. The Brother and Sister Paper Dolls were formed out of papier-mâché, then painted and decorated. These dolls, as well as the Dinosaurs, can be made from illustration board by simply following the respective templates and carefully cutting along the line with an art knife. You can then dry-mount the giftwrap in place.

You will take added pleasure in keeping old letters and cards when you store them in this unique Love-Letter Trunk. "Willow Bough" from *William Morris* is coordinated with a braided trim; roses in chromolithography adorn the front panel. A *Vienna Style* pattern inspired the costume jewelry I made. It should be noted that I painted the designs freehand on the surfaces of the bracelet and earrings; I used the design on the giftwrap as a guide for color and proportion.

Brother and Sister Paper Dolls

MATERIALS

Giftwraps by Artists: English Floral
   Patterns

*Papier-mâché (Look for a prepared medium
   in your local craft store)*

*Acrylic paints: fleshtone, yellow, brown or
   desired hair color, white, pale green,
   blue*

*Watercolor paints in tubes: peach, hot pink,
   aqua*

Fine permanent black felt-tip pen

Découpage medium

Scrap of white fabric

¼ yard of dark rose ⅝" ribbon

*Tiny dried flowers, such as baby's breath
   and everlastings*

Pencil, tracing paper

Craft knife

Cookie sheet

Metal nail file

Flat and fine, tapered paintbrushes

DIRECTIONS

1. Trace actual-size patterns onto tracing paper. Cut out along heavy outlines.

2. Prepare papier-mâché, following manufacturer's instructions on package. Press out onto cookie sheet, striving for a uniform thickness of about ¼".

3. Place cutout pattern on top, and cut around outlines. Lift pattern away.

4. Sculpting: Add a grape-size ball of papier-mâché to the bottom of each of the boy's legs, for shoes; flatten along bottom surface. In the same manner, give the girl a three-dimensional right foot. Add a small amount of papier-mâché

Actual-Size Pattern for Brother Paper Doll

around head for raised hair. Use metal file to "comb" lines into boy's hair. Use tip of file to lift up and "frizz" papier-mâché for girl's curly hair. Press a *tiny* ball of papier-mâché to center of face, for nose. Use tip of pencil to pierce nostrils into nose, and to pierce holes into head for eyes, referring to pattern for placement.

5. Let papier-mâché dry thoroughly, turning over when front is dry to let back dry.

6. Paint backs with watercolors: Girl is painted peach; boy, pale green.

7. Paint fronts as follows: First, use acrylics for base colors, referring to photo for color suggestions or using your own choices and using flat paintbrush, paint skin, clothing, and shoes. Blend light and dark tones to paint hair. With fine, tapered paintbrush, paint eyes white, let dry, then dot with blue or desired iris color. Let dry.

8. With felt-tip pen, dot irises of eyes and outline girl's eyes.

9. Using watercolor paint and fine tapered paintbrush, add details, referring to photo and pattern for placement. Paint peach cheeks, a rosy cupid's bow mouth. Scallop collars, make an aqua check pattern on boy's shirt, a fuchsia polka-dot pattern over girl's dress. Draw lines to define the girl's balloon sleeves, waistline, and folds of the skirt.

10. Découpage dress: Cut out small flowers and leaves from giftwrap. Following General Directions, apply all over dress, spacing evenly, cut motifs so they "disappear" into any folds or design lines of dress.

11. Apply two coats of découpage medium to front of figures, letting dry after each coat.

Actual-Size Pattern for Sister Paper Doll

12. For the boy, cut a 4″ x 3″ rectangle of white fabric. Coat with découpage medium. Turn long edges ¼″ to wrong side, and pinch short ends, placing one in each of boy's hands. Open out top edge to create a pouch; let dry. Découpage a tiny sprig of flowers cut from giftwrap to center top of pouch. Paint aqua dash lines across top of pouch. Fill pouch with tiny dried flowers, gluing to secure.

13. Tie a pretty bow and glue to the girl's hair.

Dinosaurs

MATERIALS

Giftwraps by Artists: American Quilts *(brontosaurus)* and Vienna Style *(stegosaurus)*

Papier-mâché (look for a prepared medium in your local craft store). Or you may substitute foamcore board to make dinosaur shapes

Découpage medium

Acrylic paint in color to coordinate with giftwrap

2 small wooden spools for each dinosaur

Cookie sheet

Flat paintbrush

Glue gun and hot-melt glue sticks

Rolling pin

Cellophane wrap

Craft knife

DIRECTIONS

1. Trace actual-size patterns. Glue to cardboard, let dry, then cut out, for templates. (If you used foamcore board instead of papier-mâché, skip Steps 2, 3, 4, and 5.)

2. Prepare papier-mâché, following manufacturer's instructions. Press or roll out with a rolling pin onto cookie sheet, striving for a uniform thickness of about ¼″. Use cellophane wrap if papier-mâché sticks to rolling pin.

3. Place template on papier-mâché and cut around with a craft knife; remove excess papier-mâché from around cutout shape. (If using foamcore instead, place template on foamcore board and work shape with pencil; cut out using sharp scissors.)

4. Let dry for at least 24 hours, then turn to the reverse side and let dry for another 24 hours, or until thoroughly dry.

5. Seal all surfaces with two coats of découpage medium, letting dry after each coat.

6. Paint edges of shape with acrylic paint; let dry.

7. Strengthen giftwrap, following General Directions on page 95. Place template on wrong side of giftwrap, and trace around. Cut out giftwrap. Turn template to the reverse side and use to cut an identical dinosaur shape from the same giftwrap.

8. Adhere giftwrap shapes to each side of papier-mâché shape, using découpage medium or to each side of foamcore board shape using dry-mount technique found in General Directions on page 95). *Note:* Giftwrap crinkles somewhat, but this adds to the primitive charm.

9. Seal entire papier-mâché shape with découpage medium. (Seal foamcore shape with 2–3 coats of lightly applied spray sealer, letting dry after each coat to each side.)

10. Hot-glue a spool centered under each leg of dinosaur. Paint spools a bright color as shown or as desired. Let dry, then seal entire piece with découpage medium.*

Note: To hasten painting and sealing procedures, thread string or insert thin dowel through hole in spool and hang. In this way, you can quickly and efficiently reach all areas.

Actual-Size Pattern for Brontosaurus

Actual-Size Pattern for Stegosaurus

Love-Letter Trunk

NOTE
Requires practice with materials

MATERIALS
Giftwraps by Artists: William Morris;
  two sheets
Double-weight illustration board
½ yard white finely woven linen fabric
Wire coat hanger
6 yards soutache braid in color to match
  giftwrap
4 yards braided cord in same color
Old-fashioned valentine or large découpage
  motif
Découpage medium
Glue gun and hot-melt glue sticks
Pencil, ruler
Tracing paper
Graphite or carbon paper
Craft knife
Wire snips and pliers

DIRECTIONS
1. From illustration board, mark and cut a rectangle 6" x 52". Set aside, for sides of box.
2. Trace actual-size quarter pattern 4 times; align dash lines and tape together to form complete pattern.
3. Using carbon or graphite paper, transfer pattern to illustration board. Cut out with craft knife and ruler, for base of trunk.
4. Select giftwrap and strengthen, following General Directions on page 95.
5. Place base on wrong side of giftwrap and trace around. Cut out giftwrap, for lining bottom of trunk.
6. Place base on illustration board and trace around. Cut out ⅛" larger all around, for lid.
7. Place lid on wrong side of giftwrap and trace around. Cut out giftwrap, for lining lid. Repeat with linen fabric, for outside of lid.
8. Prepare sides of box: Referring to diagram and General Directions for scoring, score all outward angles (dotted lines) on right side of illustration board, and all inward angles (small dash lines) on reverse side. Fold along score lines.
9. Hot-glue sides around base, keeping all bottom edges flush. Trim short edges of sides to butt, and join with hot glue.
10. Cut two 7" and two 5¾"-wide strips along entire length of giftwrap. Following General Directions, dry-mount wider strips to sides of trunk with ¼" extending at bottom and ¾" extending at top edge. Overlap edges in an inside corner if possible. Clip into excess at corners and wrap bottom edge onto bottom of base, top edge over rim and into inside of trunk. Use remaining strips to line the interior sides of the trunk.
11. Hot-glue soutache braid all around sides of trunk at top and bottom edges.
12. *Lid:* With pencil, lightly mark a line down the center of lid. Draw parallel lines ½" to either side; score along these lines.
13. Following General Directions, dry-mount linen fabric to side of lid that folds out. Fold lid at score lines to ease fabric. In same manner, dry-mount giftwrap to reverse side (underside) of lid. Hot-glue soutache braid around edges of lid, around top of lid, bypassing shaped corners as shown by scalloped line in quarter pattern, and across center, between scored lines.
14. Using sharp point such as the tip of a compass or craft knife, pierce a small hole on center line of lid, ⅝" from either end. Also pierce holes on two opposite sides of trunk, at the center of a 4" section, ⅝" below the rim.
15. *Handle:* Using wire snips, cut a 30" length of coat-hanger wire. Wrap it around a strong, large cylinder, such as a canister or column to shape it into a smooth semicircle. Insert ends into pierced holes of lid, from linen side. Using pliers, bend each wire end out for 3". Guide each end into a hole in the trunk side from the interior out. Bend wire ends up to meet handle.
16. Apply hot glue in small sections along wire, and wrap wire in tight coils with braided cord. Hot-glue ends of wire to handle, and ends of cord to secure. With remainder of cord, begin at center top of handle and wrap cord in a loose spiral, then reinforce ends with a second layer of tight coils, and bind each end to handle with a couple of wraps and a bow.
17. Glue a large découpage motif or valentine to front of trunk.

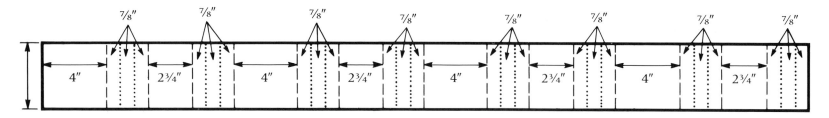

7/8" 7/8" 7/8" 7/8" 7/8" 7/8" 7/8" 7/8"

4"   2¾"   4"   2¾"   4"   2¾"   4"   2¾"

Diagram for Scoring Sides

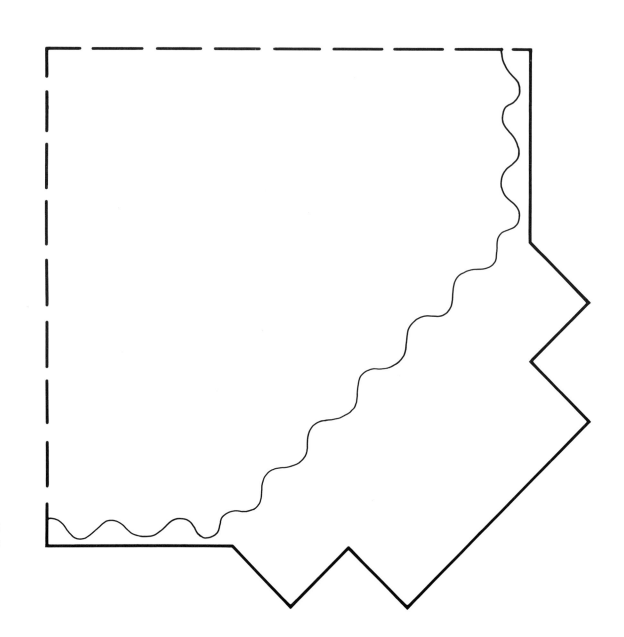

**Actual-Size Quarter Pattern
for Love-Letter Trunk**

Costume Jewelry

MATERIALS
Giftwraps by Artists: Vienna Style
Heavy cardboard
*Wooden beads: one heart ⅜" thick, 1½"
  long with hole drilled vertically through
  center plus approximately 18 12mm
  round beads, all available from Fibre
  Craft, at most local craft stores*
*Costume jewelry earrings: wire hoops or
  spirals coated with bright-colored enamel
  dangling from French back, post, or clip-
  type finding*
2 tiny wire rings for jewelry assembly
Black oil-base, quick-dry enamel paint
*Acrylic paints (these from Liquitex): Yellow
  Light, Hansan (Titanium) White, Lt.
  Blue Permanent, Lt. Portrait Pink*
Permanent black felt-tip marker
1 yard black satin cord (heavy rattail)
Glue gun and hot-melt glue sticks
Découpage medium
Clear acrylic spray sealer
Pencil, compass
Craft knife
Flat and fine, tapered paintbrushes

DIRECTIONS FOR BRACELET
1. From cardboard, mark the following pieces: two 4½" squares; four 1" x 4½" rectangles. Cut out, using either heavy-duty scissors or a ruler and craft knife.
2. On one square, mark lines across center both horizontally and vertically to locate the center. Using compass with point kept at the center and a 1¼" radius, scribe a circle. For small, slender hands, also scribe a circle with same center, and a radius of 1⅛"; for large hands, also scribe a circle with same center and a 1⅜" radius. Cut out along smallest circle first; use craft knife and turn the cardboard rather than the knife. Test-fit: hand should just fig snugly through cutout hole. If hand does not fit through hole, cut around along next largest marked circle. Test-fit and repeat if necessary. Reserve cut-out circles for earrings.
3. Place square with cutout over second square; trace circle. Cut out to form an identical shape.
4. Give all pieces of cardboard two coats of black paint on all surfaces, letting dry thoroughly between coats.
5. Assembly: Using a glue gun, run a line of glue on one square along one outer edge. Press to edge of one rectangle, with surfaces at right angles to each other. In the same manner, hot-glue a rectangle to each side of square. Join short sides of rectangles together with hot glue. You now have an open box—with a hole in the center. Hot-glue the remaining square on top, "closing" the box. (*Note:* Omit Step 6 if you are covering bracelet with giftwrap paper.)
6. Give outside surfaces of bracelet 4 to 5 more coats of black paint, letting dry after each coat.
7. Paint, découpage, or cover the bracelet. *To paint:* use the cover of *Giftwraps by Artists: Vienna Style* as a reference to work freehand over all outside surfaces of the bracelet. Use acrylic paints and a fine tapered paintbrush. Begin on one square and continue design onto adjacent surfaces. Make graceful two-tone plumes with bright colors; fill in between plumes with white squiggles, curlicues, and white or yellow dots, small and tiny. Add a few dots and squiggles to reachable areas inside bracelet. Let dry thoroughly.
To découpage: cut motifs from giftwrap and apply to bracelet, following General Directions on page 95.
8. Spray bracelet with several coats of clear sealer, letting dry after each coat on each side.

DIRECTIONS FOR EARRINGS
For each:
1. Use one of the 2½"-round cutouts from bracelet, or cut anew from cardboard, using compass to mark, craft knife to cut. Take care to cut smoothly along marked lines.
2. With a ruler, mark a light pencil line across circle, making sure to pass across depression of compass point at center. Set compass for a radius of ¹¹⁄₁₆". Place point of compass on straight line, ⅜" from exact center. Scribe a circle; carefully cut out, to form earring hoop. (See the actual-size pattern for hoop.)
3. Give hoop 6 or 7 coats of black paint on each side, letting dry after each coat.
4. Follow Step 7 for bracelet, but reduce the scale: Make plumes, squiggles and dots all smaller than those shown on cover of *Giftwraps for Artists: Vienna Style*.
5. Spray hoop with at least 2 coats of clear sealer, letting dry after each coat.
6. Using a sharp needle, pierce hoop where cutout comes closest to edge of circle, once ⅛" beyond cutout, and again ⅛" from outside edge.
7. Using tweezers or small pliers, remove the dangling enamel-coated hoop or spiral from costume jewelry earring back or finding. Insert wire from finding into outer hole of hoop. Use pliers to press wire back to secure.
8. If desired, open wire hoop and wrap around a fat pen or ½" dowel to create a

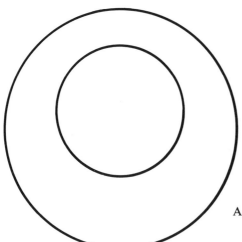

Actual-Size Pattern for Earring Hoop

small spiral that will fit inside of hoop. Wrap end of wire around a wire ring. Open ring, using tweezers or pliers, and insert one end through inner hole of painted hoop. Close up ring.

DIRECTIONS FOR NECKLACE

1. Paint heart bead with two coats of black paint, letting dry thoroughly after each coat.

2. Place wooden heart bead on cover of giftwrap book, over desired motif; trace around. Repeat for a second cardboard heart.

3. Cut out hearts slightly to the inside of traced line.

4. Using a felt-tip marker, blacken edges of cardboard hearts.

5. Using découpage medium, glue a cardboard heart to each side of heart bead, centering carefully.

6. If desired, use fine, tapered paintbrush and acrylic paints to add small motifs— swirls or dots—to fill in empty spaces on cardboard hearts.

7. Thread round beads onto household string and stretch ends of the string out taut, tying or clamping to keep string taut and horizontal. Spread beads out and paint with acrylics, varying the colors.

8. Spray beads with several coats of acrylic sealer, letting dry after each coat.

9. To string beads for necklace, begin by making a tight knot 7″ from one end of satin cord. Working from the other end, slip on a round bead, passing it all the way to the knot. Tie another knot on other side of bead to secure. Add three more round beads, varying colors and following each bead with a knot. Next, thread cord through top of heart bead and tie a knot following heart. String on remaining beads in same manner as before. Bring ends of cord together and tie a knot, dabbing with glue to prevent knot from slipping.

General Directions

CHOOSING A GIFTWRAP PATTERN

Many designs from the various *Giftwraps by Artists* books may be used with beautiful results. Open your book and select a giftwrap. Tear out the sheet along perforated dash lines. Unfold the sheet vertically and horizontally to its full dimension: 18¾" x 27", and smooth creases.

TO PREPARE GIFTWRAP FOR CRAFTS PROJECTS

Giftwraps by Artists is a high-quality but lightweight paper. I recommend strengthening the giftwrap, particularly before adhering it to another surface.

To Use Spray Sealer

Unfold the sheet and place in a *very well ventilated* area. Read directions for clear acrylic spray sealer and take all necessary precautions. Spray one side of giftwrap. Let dry for about 15 minutes, then turn to the wrong side and spray again. Let dry. For dry-mounting, this process should be repeated 4 to 5 times.

To Laminate

Lay a clear, self-adhesive plastic such as Con-Tact Brand flat on your work surface, paper side up. Peel away the paper backing. Keep the giftwrap folded into quarters as it comes in the book; place one-quarter (printed side down) on the adhesive plastic; strive to line up side edges at least approximately. Smooth along the surface of the giftwrap. Unfold the giftwrap once, and smooth down, then unfold the giftwrap the rest of the way and smooth. Avoid using hot-melt glue with laminated surfaces.

TO USE A CRAFT KNIFE

Work with a slim-handled, good-quality craft knife, such as an X-ACTO knife. Place giftwrap on a protected surface. Turn paper so you are always cutting toward you. Change blades whenever knife starts to drag and does not cut cleanly through paper. Use a metal-edge ruler to cut straight lines, a T- or carpenter's square to ensure right angles.

To score, use a ruler and craft knife but cut only partway through cardboard or illustration board. Scoring provides a fold line; fold away from the cut side.

TO DÉCOUPAGE

Use a craft knife or a small, sharp scissors to cut out a motif from strengthened giftwrap. Plan your arrangement on a background, then put motif aside. Using a flat brush, apply a very thin coat of Mod Podge or other découpage medium to the background. Reposition motif on top. Working from the center of the motif outward, press in place, smoothing out any air bubbles. Use the tip of a craft knife or small knitting needle to press down tiny pieces, holding them in place until they adhere. Let dry. Brush a thin coat of découpage medium over entire surface. Let dry thoroughly. If surface shows brushstrokes, rub lightly with a very fine garnet paper or sandpaper, and dust with a tack cloth. Repeat with one or two coats of découpage medium. Spray entire piece with clear acrylic sealer.

TO DRY-MOUNT GIFTWRAP

Strengthen giftwrap as described above. Apply a thin, even coat of rubber cement or apply a spray adhesive such as 3M's Spray-Mount to the wrong side of both the giftwrap and the surface to be covered. (I prefer rubber cement in most cases because it doesn't buckle or wrinkle the giftwrap.) Let dry a few moments until rubber cement or adhesive is tacky to the touch. Place giftwrap over surface, positioning it as desired. Press it down, working from the center outward in all directions to remove and/or prevent air bubbles. If you are dissatisfied with the placement, you may carefully lift giftwrap and reposition it.

TO USE A HOT-GLUE GUN

The glue gun dispenses a hot adhesive which bonds almost immediately and dries in seconds. Its main advantage is its speed in securing items where you want them, without clamping, tacking, or taping. It is convenient, neat, easy, and safe—if you follow the manufacturer's instructions. Don't use a glue gun with laminated giftwrap, as the hot glue will melt the self-adhesive plastic.

Giftwraps by Artists

Drawing upon great traditions in graphic design and the work of great individual artists, these wrapping-paper books reproduce classic patterns in a delightful blend of art and utility.

Every volume in the *Giftwraps by Artists* series contains 16 sheets of wrapping paper bound into a book, each folded twice and perforated for neat removal. Each sheet of wrapping paper is thus four times the size of the book: 18¾ x 27". If these giftwraps are not available in your local bookshop or gift store, write to the following address for information on how to obtain them.

Harry N. Abrams, Inc.
Attn: Special Sales Dept.
100 Fifth Avenue
New York, N.Y. 10011

William Morris
Vienna Style
Raoul Dufy
Kimono: Japanese Designs
American Quilts
English Floral Patterns
M. C. Escher
Paisley
Art Nouveau: Paris 1895
French Flowers: Nineteenth-
    Century Textile Designs
Art Deco: Holiday Designs
Neoclassical Designs